Ideologies

The purpose of this series is to demonstrate, through the treatment of problems drawn from contemporary life, the practical relevance of philosophy. The aim is to show how philosophical problems can arise out of, and can exert a profound influence upon, our personal and social problems; and how philosophical analysis can enlighten our moral attitudes, aspirations and decisions. At the same time, since the authors all in fact belong to the liberal, empiricist tradition of British thought, their attempts to show philosophy at work are also attempts to re-express, in a form that fits the time, the liberal vision of man and society.

PHILOSOPHY AT WORK

General Editor: Patrick Corbett
*Professor of Philosophy
at the University of Sussex*

Ideologies

PATRICK CORBETT

*Professor of Philosophy
at the University of Sussex*

HUTCHINSON OF LONDON

HUTCHINSON & CO *(Publishers)* LTD
178–202 Great Portland Street, London W.1

London Melbourne Sydney
Auckland Bombay Toronto
Johannesburg New York

First published 1965

This book has been set in Pilgrim,
printed in Great Britain on Antique Wove paper
by The Anchor Press, Ltd., and bound by
Wm. Brendon & Son Ltd., both of Tiptree, Essex

Contents

First Remarks:
Conflict of Ideas

THIS book is about the theories that men form as to what they are and what they should be—in a word, as to their free-dom. It starts from the fact that men can be so divided in their views of freedom that they can no longer trust or work with one another. They can even cease to wish to do so, and only hanker to destroy.

This fact is remarkable; to those who live in divided coun-tries it is also painfully familiar. The citizen of Poland or Vietnam, of Bengal or South Africa, is not likely to forget it; he spends much of his life confronted by its consequences. But if birds of a feather flock together, so do men of one opinion; chattering constantly together in identical tones of voice, they have no ear for any other. Thus, in a country like England, where the obliteration of intellectual differences is a developed art, wars of ideas are so unfamiliar as almost to be incredible; so much so that this book would never have been written but for certain experiences, of which these are typical.

In the autumn of 1940 I was in solitary confinement in a German military prison. The days were long; so when a friendly sergeant on night-duty offered to let me out of my cell of an evening for a talk I accepted with alacrity. We had several conversations and, both being university men, we seemed at first to find some common interests. About Goethe and Shakespeare we could talk in quite a friendly, useful way. But on current affairs we could get nowhere. He was as convinced a Nazi as I was a convinced liberal; he thought it right and proper, I thought it monstrous, to persecute the Jews; he believed in leadership and order, I in democracy and discussion; he took his stand on race, I on universal human values; each found his own arguments clear and compelling, the other's muddled and absurd. So while we had met as

7

fellow-men, despite our uniforms, we parted as embittered foes; each thought the other only fit to die.

Ruins are still standing in the empty centre of Berlin. Even now the air there seems to smell of burning; one only wants to get away, either to the east or to the west, where there is life, and work, and talk. And, up to a point, the life on each side is the same. On each side people are born and die; they suffer and enjoy on much the same occasions; they work with much the same techniques; and, as for talk, if you asked on either side about the weather, or the structure of the atom, or the dates of the two world wars, or a thousand other factual matters, you would be given the same answer. On each side people are lucid or cool, dull or amusing, irrespective of their political opinions. But if you go to and fro across the city and ask questions about political parties, or the present power of ex-Nazis, or comparative industrial development and standards of living, or refugees, or churches, the answers that are poured out over you from either side seem to have no common element but hatred of the other. Seen from the East, the West is crypto-fascist; seen from the West, the East is red; and that is that. You can find no argument to adjust—not even to begin to adjust—the one side to the other, no way to soften their harsh emotions. As you sit down and listen, first to one, then to the other, you can do nothing but make sure that the two speakers, though monsters in each other's eyes, are men in yours.

But it is not necessary, even for an Englishman, to go abroad for such experiences; even in comfortable England they are available in milder forms. Liberal-minded people believe that rules of conduct, essential as they are, should be applied flexibly and with charity. As a rule, one should tell the truth, but not when doing so hurts feelings to no purpose; as a rule, one should promote one's country's interests, but not when modest gain for it involves disaster for another. Casting around for an expression of this thought one may light on Jesus's parable of the good Samaritan: the story of the man who crossed the road to help another man in trouble when the strict keepers of rules and watchers of their interests had walked past, with eyes averted, on the other side. This story is as eloquent to a liberal-minded atheist as to any Christian; the message of equality that it bears to him is clear and sound. Suppose, then, that the atheist takes occasion to discuss this point of morals with a Christian and finds that for all practical purposes they agree on what it means. They see eye to eye, and would act together. But then the Christian says that for him this moral conviction is inseparable from that Christian faith of his, which, to the atheist, is senseless. There they are. They are both men. They share completely, for all practical purposes, what both regard as this most important of convictions, that one should not be hidebound by one's rules or interests; yet what the Christian believes to be indispensable to this conviction the atheist asserts to be irrelevant. The misunderstanding is complete. Now, given all the circumstances, this is not, of course, one of those conflicts of ideas that is likely to lead to civil war or persecution. Christian and atheistic Englishmen of this day and age share too many interests and convictions to resort to force. But their difference is no less puzzling for that, and could conceivably become as destructive in the future as it has been in the past.

For there is nothing new about ideological conflict; it is as old as religion itself. The faithful have struggled with one another in the names of their faiths all down the ages, just as they are doing now. What is new in our time is that the faiths for which men seek life and destroy it have become more social than religious in their inspiration, and that men's powers of destruction have become so great as to threaten the existence not merely of the chosen victims but of all mankind.

Every man must always ask himself, however casually and faintly: What am I? What should I be? In what joint faith should we proceed? But each of us now faces this question too: How are we to think about faith in the age of the hydrogen bomb?

We face this question together, but we can only come to grips with it from our own positions. We must all recognise that, however necessary our faith is to ourselves, we can no longer seek to impose it on other men by force; we must all accept the fact that faiths must now live side by side in peace; we must all find a way of holding our own faith tolerantly; but each must do this for himself, in his own style, and setting out from where he stands. It would be idiotically pretentious for anyone to try to speak, at once, for all; in this matter, to try to state common principles forthwith is to be left with empty platitudes. Much better than that is to be as candid as we can about ourselves.

To be candid, then: this book is written by a man without religion. I do not believe in any kind of God, or any kind of spirit, or any kind of immortality. Man, for me, is just an unusually intelligent and sensitive kind of animal; sprinkled through the universe there are, no doubt, a lot of others. But if I lack religious faith I lack social faith as well. I do not believe that this human animal is naturally progressive, with an inherent and irresistible tendency to self-perfection built into his physical or social nature: we are capable of catastrophe. Rather, I am a hopeful sceptic. Looking at my own existence, I find a few decades of life sufficient in themselves; there is, for me, full splendour in the onward pace of time. And looking at the existences of others, now alive or to be born, I do not need elaborate argument to be convinced that human knowledge, power, activity, and pleasure should be increased as much, and shared as equally, as possible. Doing better now is what I care for, not a perfected future life, whether in heaven or on earth.

But while the more elaborate theories professed by many of my neighbours—Marxists and Catholics, for example— have no hold upon me as convictions, they fascinate me as phenomena, and interest me as suggestions. I like to have them pressed upon me from the hustings or the pulpit; to see things, for a moment, through their eyes; to feel their characteristic passions stir within my heart. I want to understand them; to do them all the justice that I can, within the shifting limits of my own position; and—since it seems unreasonable to suppose that the theories of men like Marx and Aquinas are all rot—to profit by whatever truth they may contain. Finally, since force, which has been a chief means of change throughout the human past, has now become so intolerably dangerous that we men must find out how to live and change together without recourse to it, I hope to contribute something to the art of moderating intellectual conflict and taming the embattled mind.

How should this enquiry start? It seems obvious that it will be useful to have before us right away—even in brief and simplified forms—some typical specimens of the kind of theory that concerns us. But if we are to approach them in the spirit of the last four paragraphs it will also be useful to pause a moment first in order to consider the word which is commonly used to denote this kind of theory nowadays, and which has therefore been chosen as the title of this book. Verbal matters are not always trivial; in the letter lives the spirit.

It is obvious, when one comes to think of it, that the word 'ideology', unlike, for example, the words 'two' or 'hat', does not possess a clear and settled meaning on which all its users are agreed. In everybody's mouth the term refers to systems of belief about human conduct; but as to what kinds of system and belief and conduct are to be included under it, and what excluded, opinions vary. Some people are prepared to regard a few sentences—the Apostolic Creed, for instance—as enough to constitute an ideology; others think of something more complex. Some say that the beliefs that constitute an ideology may be rational; others apply the word only to beliefs they deem illusions, so that the term is for them intrinsically hostile. Some call religious beliefs ideological; others restrict the term to political beliefs alone. Such divergencies in the use of words are common. Taking only the words that were used in the last paragraph, 'religious' and 'rational' are equally diverse in usage. Is Marxism a religion? Or Voodoo? Or Zen? Is art a rational activity? Or criticism? Or theology? Good reasons can be given for either answer to any of these questions; and that means that the key terms are used in different ways on different occasions. Now while such diversities are quite harmless so long as they are recognised, they are always liable to give rise to misunderstanding and unprofitable argument; for when people unwittingly use words in different senses their arguments and disagreements are liable to become verbal, in the bad sense of that term, while the issues of substance are not faced. So when we are confronted, as in this case, by a wide variety of vaguely similar phenomena, which can properly be classified in different ways, for different purposes, everybody must decide and explain how he will use the word— within broad limits of what will be comprehensible and convenient to others—and then stick to his proposal.

The usage that I propose for 'ideology' in this book is this. First, the word will carry no implication that what it denotes is good, bad, or indifferent; there is, consequently, no implication as to the rationality of the beliefs to which the word refers. Second, no restriction will be imposed upon the content of the beliefs that make up the ideology; on this usage ideologies may therefore be moral, religious, or political, or these and any others mixed together. Third, the term will imply that the beliefs referred to, taken together, should have important implications for a wide range of conduct; to accept the ideology is to be committed to a way of life. Fourth, the term will imply that some of the beliefs concern the general nature of man and of the world he lives in; for example, that the world is ultimately spiritual in nature. Fifth, the term will imply that the beliefs referred to constitute a system in the minimal sense that they are asserted by those who hold them to support each other, and the way of life, and are used by them to do so. And, finally, the term will imply that the system of beliefs should be associated with some institution, class, or social group in such a regular way that the holding of these beliefs by an individual is a condition of his membership of the body in question.

On this usage, Gandhism, Catholicism, Leninism, Nazism, American Democracy, and the Divine Right of Kings are, or were, ideologies; and so, on a smaller scale, are the myths of English Public Schools or Amazonian tribes. The Theory of Relativity is not, since it has no implications for conduct; the view that capital punishment is wrong, taken by itself, is not, since it bears on one segment of conduct only; a code of professional conduct is not, since, although it may affect a considerable range of conduct, it does not explicitly comprise beliefs about the general nature of man and the world; and anti-semitism (at least in England, at the present time) is not, since, although it may have all the other characteristics, it is not explicitly associated, as a kind of badge, with any definite social group. By 'ideology', therefore, is meant here any intellectual structure consisting of: a set of beliefs about the conduct of life and the organisation of society; a set of beliefs about man's nature and the world in which he lives; a claim that the two sets are interdependent; and a demand that those beliefs should be professed, and that claim conceded, by anyone who is to be considered a full member of a certain social group. (An ideologist will therefore be a man who makes it his business to put such structures forward.) Whether, in any one case or in all cases, the beliefs in question are as meaningful as they are claimed to be; whether, if *meaningful, they are sound or unsound; whether their alleged interdependence is genuine or spurious; and whether making their profession a badge of group membership is realistic or artificial: all these issues are left open by this definition. The word being vague, other definitions may be better for other purposes; this neutral one is the best for ours.*

And now, with an attitude of constructive curiosity embodied in this crucial word, I suggest that we listen to some typical ideologists, as they might well speak, or as they actually have spoken: first a Marxist, then a Catholic, then an American democrat. How their speeches have been composed is explained in the note at the end of the volume.

PART ONE

THREE
IDEOLOGISTS
SPEAK

I

The Marxist

THE issue before us is that of the liberation of man. The time has come when men can free themselves from the age-old frustrations of ignorance, poverty, and oppression, moving forward into an epoch in which each individual, master of his fate at last, can lead, in equality and peace, a full, harmonious, and creative life. But in order to understand this prospect and play our part in its achievement we must discard many old illusions and see things as they really are. We must look at the material world with the eyes of science, and then follow the development of humanity in the same objective way. And we must always remember that the aim of our enquiry is not merely theoretical: we seek knowledge for the sake of freedom. Hitherto philosophers have only interpreted the world in various ways; the point, however, is to change it.

When we look outward with the eye of science what is given to us first of all is the world of inanimate matter, stretching away into the infinities of space and time. This material world is its own cause; there is no sense in looking for a further cause outside itself; to tell a story of divine creation is to lapse from science into fancy. And it is this material world, existing independently of any mind, finite or infinite, that is given to us in sense experience. Of course, very little of its nature is directly given; to discover the complexity of its structure and the course of its development innumerable experiences must be brought together into generalisations, and these generalisations must be tested by the result of acting on them. The fruit of this enquiry, at once practical and theoretical in nature and stretching, in one form or another, over the whole of human history, is the picture of the world produced by modern science. This picture is developing at an unprecedented speed; but, so far as it goes at any moment, it is now of unprecedented accuracy. Far more than any men before us we see nature as it is.

In investigating the world in which we live, however, we have not only found that things happen in the regular connected ways that science sets before us; we have found that the world itself develops. Nature is not merely repetitive; it brings forth new things; it grows. Such growth has no doubt taken place, and is still taking place, throughout the universe; however, the growth that particularly concerns us is that which has taken place on the surface of this earth. Here we can follow through the eyes of science the ways in which matter has assumed more and more complicated forms, in the course of which quite new qualities have come into existence. Most notably: inanimate matter begins to live and feel; the animal and the human mind emerge. These minds are neither reducible to physical properties nor separable from physical things. Organic and mental life are higher forms of the organisation of matter, higher forms that come into existence as bodies reach successive levels of complexity. In this emergence of the mind, as in the emergence of other novel qualities, there is no ultimate mystery. Science is constantly probing deeper into the ways in which such innovations come about; but meanwhile we must just take it as a fact that come about they do. We gain no more from mythical accounts of the origin of the mind than we do from mythical accounts of the origin of the solar system. To say that the world was made by a spiritual and rational God and that man has those qualities because God, as a unique privilege, gave them to him: that is to bemuse oneself with words. What we want is proper scientific explanation, not empty metaphysics. How then, plainly and empirically, have we men become what we now are?

For a clear understanding of the physical basis of mind we have still to wait. Genetics and neurology, cybernetics and psychology, are making great strides forward; sometime in the next half-century we shall unravel the immensely complicated organisations of matter that give rise to thought and feeling. At the same time we shall discover how these organisations are handed down from one generation to another. But for the present we must take all that for granted, concentrating on what can be understood already: on man's

social development, and on the ways in which that development has given rise to particular forms of human life and
thought and feeling, whatever their ultimate physical basis
may be.

To this end we must begin by recognising the first pre-
supposition of all human existence, namely that men must
be in a position to satisfy their physical needs in order to be
able to make history. Now, while men can be distinguished
from animals by circumstances, by religion or by anything
one likes, they, for their part, distinguish themselves from
animals as soon as they begin to produce their means of
subsistence, a step which is determined by their physical
constitution. Man is, first and foremost, a productive animal.
He does not merely take and consume such material means
of life as the world around him offers; he uses parts of the
world around him to create means of life which otherwise
would not exist at all. He turns stones into hammers and
logs into boats. And while, at first, men to a great extent remained mere gatherers of food and users of natural imple-
ments and shelters, so that production was a secondary
factor in their lives, in course of time they came to depend
upon production more and more until they could not survive without it. This development of man's productive
powers is the real basis of his history.

Before considering this in detail it is necessary to establish
what that phrase 'real basis' means. Here again we must stick
to the facts. If we look at social change two things stand out.
The first is that through all failures and interruptions men
have searched for more efficient ways of producing their
material means of life; the second is that when such means
are discovered they are eventually adopted, even when it is
difficult to do so. Recent history clearly illustrates both
these assertions. The world is seething with technological
discovery; and no society, however ancient and settled its
form of life, has been able to stand aside from the process of
technological revolution which gathered momentum in
Europe two to three hundred years ago. Neither tradition, nor
religion, nor the entrenched interests of old regimes and
classes, can stand against the universal demand for higher
productivity: that is a truth that can no longer be denied.
But what lies behind it? Surely the truth is that men are so
constituted that the demands that they make upon their

environment are immensely greater than they have ever been able to satisfy by production. Man has always lived in the shadow of his vast unsatisfied desire for goods. It is that desire that has driven him on to seek out and adopt new techniques of production. In this ceaseless quest for the intellectual and practical mastery of nature, pursued both for its own sake and for that of satisfying his demand for goods, we reach the bedrock of man's nature. This, whatever may be its explanation in physical terms, is the fundamental human impulse; only in relation to it can the past, present, and future of mankind be understood.

History is nothing but the activity of men in pursuit of their ends; there is no order or pattern of history over and above the real, living, active, individual man and woman. But once we have recognised the mastery of nature as the overriding human impulse we can begin to see why it is that men, in pursuit of their aims, have acted as they have, and come to live as they do. And not only can we unravel the mystery of the human past; we discover the structure and tendencies of the human present. That means that henceforward we shall be able to pursue the mastery of nature with a clear understanding of the human factors involved, and so with more effect. Indeed, men have now reached a stage in the development of their intellectual and productive powers at which further progress is only possible if they do achieve realistic insight into their social being. A philosophical revolution must complete the scientific and industrial relolution upon which Western Europe and capitalism launched the world. But to prepare for that revolution we must follow in more detail the development of Promethean man.

From the moment that man begins to live by production rather than by just consuming what nature offers, the means of production become essential to him. Instead of taking nature as it comes, he works upon it; he turns stones into tools, forest into fields, trees into logs, changing them, that is, in such a way that he can go on to use them to produce his food or shelter. But once he finds that he can only get adequate food or shelter by using such means of production, his life comes really to depend upon them and, whether collectively or individually, he must keep them for his own. The whole organisation of society thus begins to turn upon the material means without whose use it would literally die.

The relationship of men to their means of production becomes the decisive factor in their lives. All other human relationships—sexual relationships, for example, or the relationships between societies—become subject to the primordial necessity of maintaining, using, and replacing the material means of production. And when we take into account the fact that men are manifestly compelled by their constitution not only to produce, but to produce more, we can see that that primordial necessity is not only one of maintaining, using, and replacing, but also of transforming and inventing the material means of life. It is this that makes intelligible the course of human history. Man's insatiable demands on nature always drive him forward; but he is not free to take any step at any time; on the contrary, he can only do what his existing means of production permit. They must be kept in being; if they are to be replaced they must be used to produce the replacement. The range of human possibility is restricted at any time by what men have already done—by the sum of what remains of old productive efforts embodied in his tools and huts and fields. The rise and fall of forms of social life are unintelligible until we learn to string them on the thread of man's productive power and its physical embodiments.

In the earliest stages of its growth different individuals may perhaps have had no special skills. If it is merely a question of using a stick to knock down fruit everyone can do the work for himself. But special skills were then developed. It was discovered that more and better goods could be produced if different individuals, families, or groups specialised their productive work in one direction or another. The life of labour on which men entered when they started to produce became a life of divided, specialised labour, a life involving, therefore, the exchange of goods produced. As men became more powerful, so they also became more dependent on each other and upon the growing apparatus by whose use they exercised their skills.

One phenomenon stands out amongst all those that mark the millennia between tribal life and modern industrial society: the phenomenon of social class, the division of mankind into the leisurely rich and the labouring poor. How did human society come to be split in this remarkable way? To take one example: in a dry country irrigation channels are amongst the most important instruments of production. It may sometimes be possible for man to do his own irrigation; normally, however, the work requires co-operation; frequently the co-operation has to be on a large scale, a scale so large as to be beyond the organisational power of independent producers, or even of small groups. When the stage has been set by circumstances in this sort of way it becomes necessary for the survival and development of society that ownership and control of the essential means of production should pass out of the hands of those who work directly with them into the hands of a minority who can supply the organisation that is needed. Thenceforward society is necessarily divided into classes, and essentially into two classes: the masters of the means of production and those who work for them as their slaves, serfs, or employees.

The characteristics of these classes and their relations to each other are determined by the same facts that gave rise to the division. The societies in question were or are poor. Their science is rudimentary; their technology is primitive; their stock of productive instruments is small. Whatever ideals of justice anyone might hold it is therefore impossible for more than a small minority to enjoy the resources that are needed for an educated, cultivated, leisured life. The great majority are condemned, simply by the economic weakness of society, to lead a life of extreme poverty and brutalising toil. The picture is not pleasant, but it is no use adopting a moralistic attitude towards it. However great the exploitation and suffering involved, class society is a phase through which man had to go before he could do better. The minority who organise society must also be its prime beneficiaries; the majority who labour cannot be anything else but poor. And since this exploited majority must resent their exploitation and hate their exploiters the most striking feature of class society is the growth of organised force—law, police, armies, officials, in fact the whole apparatus of the state—designed to keep them in position. But man cannot live by force alone. There remains deep in the human conscience the sense that class society, however unavoidable, is ultimately wrong. It follows that being obliged to live divided into classes, men had to try to conceal the facts of that situation from themselves, or at least to render them more palatable. This was the function of religion, which, besides

filling up with magical explanations the vast areas of fact
into which scientific thinking had not begun to penetrate,
consoled the poor for their sufferings in the present with
promises of a better world to come, and assured the rich
that everything was as it should be because the gods had
made it so.

Such ideological disguises could not, however, prevent
men from feeling the pressure of scarcity and looking for
improvements. The history of man since he left the tribal
state is the history of class struggles: the struggles of the
exploited against their exploiters, and the struggles of new
kinds of exploiter against the old. The first kind of struggle
was always doomed to failure. So long as the economic conditions of class society remained it was impossible for slaves
or serfs to throw off their oppressors. Revolts begun in despair ended in slaughter. Economic conditions dictated that
the many must be ruled by the few, and that the few should
enjoy but the many suffer. It simply was not possible for the
toiling majority of mankind, however bitter and detestable
their lot, to institute a different order. Some new factor had
to enter on the scene before a change could come. And the
change eventually came through the emergence of a new
kind of exploiter. The origins, function and character of a
ruling class is always determined by its economic role; so
long as the prime needs of life are scarce, those who control
production rule the world. But under the remorseless pressure
of scarcity, as we have seen, men have always been looking
for ways to improve their situation, for new methods of
production more effective than the old. Sometimes such new
methods of production have been introduced and adopted
by an existing ruling class; but in virtue of the inherent conservatism of classes what has happened much more often is
that the new methods of production have been developed by
a new class, which, by establishing them, stakes its claims to
power and eventually ousts its less productive predecessor.
This is what happened in Europe as the Middle Ages gave
place to the modern world. New developments in science,
new technologies, and new systems of production, all far
more effective than the old, were brought into existence by
the rising bourgeoisie. The political history of Europe for
several centuries consisted in the efforts of this new class to
establish itself against its feudal predecessors. In the

end it was successful; it had to be so because its productive resources were immensely superior. Steam and machinery were irresistible. Kings and aristocracies were swept aside, churches and empires were overrun; whole continents were populated. Capitalism, with its factories, mines, and steamships, did what no other power could do before: it brought the world together. But remarkable as these developments were, their full significance can only be understood in the light of what was to happen next. Capitalist society has two sides. On the one hand it has not only brought into existence far greater productive powers than men have ever known before, but has discovered a complicated technique of increasing these powers with immense speed; on the other hand, it, like other forms of class society, has caused great suffering to the majority of people in all those societies where it has prevailed. While it has given men, in modern science and technology, the means by which the scarcity from which they have suffered hitherto can finally be conquered, it has also inflicted upon men sufferings as great as any they have endured before. And these two sides of capitalism are linked together in the shape of the industrial proletariat. The conquest of poverty is only possible through mass production, and mass production is only possible by the creation of a new class of urban factory worker. This class has been exploited by capitalists as much as serfs were by their feudal lords. Only by this exploitation could the bourgeoisie create the gigantic capital resources by means of which the conquest of poverty could eventually be undertaken. But while capitalism has brought these resources into existence it cannot really use them. There is a fundamental contradiction between private ownership of the means of production and the full use of those means for the satisfaction of human needs. Leaving aside the precise nature of these contradictions their reality is proved by the periodic slumps, with all their waste and unemployment, more generally by the underemployment of resources, to which capitalism seems to be inherently subjective. As in the previous cases, what is happening here is that the institutions of a particular ruling class are no longer fitted to contain and develop the productive resources which have come to exist in society; hence the institutions have got to go.

This contradiction is of such primordial importance for

the present and future of mankind that we must dwell on it at greater length: only so can we grasp the slavery of the present and the freedom of the future.

In capitalistic society the means of production can only function when they have undergone a preliminary transformation into capital, into the means of exploiting human labour-power. The necessity of this transformation into capital of the means of production and subsistence stands like a ghost between these and the workers. It alone prevents the coming together of the material and personal levers of production; it alone forbids the means of production to function, the workers to work and live. On the one hand, therefore, the capitalistic mode of production stands convicted of its own incapacity to further direct these productive forces. On the other, these productive forces themselves, with increasing energy, press forward to the removal of the existing contradiction, to the abolition of their quality as capital, to the *practical recognition of their character as social productive forces*.

This rebellion of the productive forces, as they grow more and more powerful, against their quality as capital, this stronger and stronger command that their social character shall be recognised, forces the capitalist class itself to treat them more and more as social productive forces, so far as this is possible under capitalist conditions. The period of industrial high pressure, with its unbounded inflation of credit, not less than the crash itself, by the collapse of great capitalist establishments, tends to bring about that form of the socialisation of great masses of means of production which we meet with in the different kinds of joint-stock companies. Many of these means of production and of distribution are, from the outset, so colossal that, like the railways, they exclude all other forms of capitalistic exploitation. At a further stage of evolution this form also becomes insufficient. The producers on a large scale in a particular branch of industry in a particular country unite in a 'Trust', a union for the purpose of regulating production. They determine the total amount to be produced, parcel it out among themselves, and thus enforce the selling price fixed beforehand.

In the trusts freedom of competition changes into its very opposite—into monopoly; and the production without any definite plan of capitalistic society capitulates to the production upon a definite plan of the invading socialistic society. Certainly this is so far still to the benefit and advantage of the capitalists. But in this case the exploitation is so palpable that it must break down. No nation will put up with production conducted by trusts with so barefaced an exploitation of the community by a small band of dividend-mongers.

In any case, with trusts or without, the official representative of capitalist society—the state—will ultimately have to undertake the direction of production. This necessity for conversion into state property is felt first in the great institutions for intercourse and communication—the post office, the telegraphs, the railways.

If the crises demonstrate the incapacity of the bourgeoisie for managing any longer modern productive forces the transformation of the great establishments for production and distribution into joint-stock companies, trusts, and state property show how unnecessary the bourgeoisie are for that purpose. All the social functions of the capitalist are now performed by salaried employees. The capitalist has no further social function than that of pocketing dividends, tearing off coupons, and gambling on the Stock Exchange, where the different capitalists despoil one another of their capital. At first the capitalistic mode of production forces out the workers. Now it forces out the capitalists, and reduces them, just as it reduced the workers, to the ranks of the surplus population, although not immediately into those of the industrial reserve army.

But the transformation, either into joint-stock companies and trusts, or into state-ownership, does not do away with the capitalistic nature of the productive forces. In the joint-stock companies and trusts this is obvious. And the modern state, again, is only the organisation that bourgeois society takes on in order to support the external conditions of the capitalist mode of production against the encroachments as well of the workers as of individual capitalists. The modern state, no matter what its form, is essentially a capitalist machine, the state of the capitalists, the ideal personification of the total national capital. The more it proceeds to the taking over of productive forces, the more does it actually become the national capitalist, the more citizens

does it exploit. The workers remain wage-workers—proletarians. The capitalist relation is not done away with. It is rather
brought to a head. But, brought to a head, it topples over.
State-ownership of the productive forces is not the solution
of the conflict, but concealed within it are the technical conditions that form the elements of that solution.

This solution can only consist in the practical recognition
of the social nature of the modern forces of production, and
therefore in the harmonising of the modes of production,
appropriation, and exchange with the socialised character
of the means of production. And this can only come about
by society openly and directly taking possession of the productive forces which have outgrown all control except that
of society as a whole. The social character of the means of
production and of the products today reacts against the
producers, periodically disrupts all production and exchange,
acts only like a law of nature working blindly, forcibly,
destructively. But with the taking over by society of the
productive forces, the social character of the means of production and of the products will be utilised by the producers
with a perfect understanding of its nature, and instead of
being a source of disturbance and periodical collapse, will
become the most powerful lever of production itself.

Active social forces work exactly like natural forces:
blindly, forcibly, destructively, so long as we do not understand, and reckon with, them. But when once we understand
them, when once we grasp their action, their direction, their
effects, it depends only upon ourselves to subject them more
and more to our own will, and by means of them to reach
our own ends. And this holds quite especially of the mighty
productive forces of today. As long as we obstinately refuse
to understand the nature and the character of these social
means of action—and this understanding goes against the
grain of the capitalist mode of production and its defenders
—so long these forces are at work in spite of us, in opposition to us, so long they master us, as we have shown above
in detail.

But when once their nature is understood they can, in the
hands of the producers working together, be transformed
from master demons into willing servants. The difference
is as that between the destructive force of electricity in the
lightning of the storm and electricity under command in the

telegraph and the voltaic arc; the difference between a conflagration and fire working in the service of man. With this recognition, at last, of the real nature of the productive forces of today the social anarchy of production gives place to a social regulation of production upon a definite plan, according to the needs of the community and of each individual. Then the capitalist mode of appropriation, in which the product enslaves first the producer and then the appropriator, is replaced by the mode of appropriation of the products that is based upon the nature of the modern means of production; upon the one hand, direct social appropriation, as means to the maintenance and extension of production—on the other, direct individual appropriation, as means of subsistence and of enjoyment.

Whilst the capitalist mode of production more and more completely transforms the great majority of the population into proletarians, it creates the power which, under penalty of its own destruction, is forced to accomplish this revolution. Whilst it forces on more and more the transformation of the vast means of production, already socialised, into state property, it shows itself the way to accomplishing this revolution. *The proletariat seizes political power and turns the means of production into state property.*

But in doing this it abolishes itself as proletariat, abolishes all class distinctions and class antagonisms, abolishes also the state as state. Society thus far, based upon class antagonisms, had need of the state. That is, of an organisation of the particular class which was *pro tempore* the exploiting class, an organisation for the purpose of preventing any interference from without with the existing conditions of production, and, therefore, especially, for the purpose of forcibly keeping the exploited classes in the condition of oppression corresponding with the given mode of production (slavery, serfdom, wage-labour). The state was the official representative of society as a whole; the gathering of it together into a visible embodiment. But it was this only in so far as it was the state of that class which itself represented, for the time being, society as a whole : in ancient times the state of slave-owning citizens; in the Middle Ages the feudal lords; in our own time the bourgeoisie. When at last it becomes the real representative of the whole of society it renders itself unnecessary. As soon as there is no longer any social class to be

held in subjection; as soon as class rule, and the individual
struggle for existence based upon our present anarchy in
production, with the collisions and excesses arising from
these, are removed, nothing more remains to be repressed,
and a special repressive force, a state, is no longer necessary.
The first act by virtue of which the state really constitutes
itself the representative of the whole of society—the taking
possession of the means of production in the name of society
—this is, at the same time, its last independent act as a state.
State interference in social relations becomes, in one domain
after another, superfluous, and then dies out of itself; the
government of persons is replaced by the administration of
things, and by the conduct of processes of production. The
state is not 'abolished'. *It dies out.* This gives the measure of
the value of the phrase 'a free state', both as to its justifiable
use at times by agitators, and as to its ultimate scientific
insufficiency; and also of the demands of the so-called anarch-
ists for the abolition of the state out of hand.

Since the historical appearance of the capitalist mode of
production the appropriation by society of all the means of
production has often been dreamed of, more or less vaguely,
by individuals as well as by sects, as the ideal of the future.
But it could become possible, could become a historical
necessity, only when the actual conditions for its realisation
were there. Like every other social advance it becomes prac-
ticable not by men understanding that the existence of
classes is in contradiction to justice, equality, etc., not by
the mere willingness to abolish these classes, but by virtue
of certain new economic conditions. The separation of
society into an exploiting and an exploited class, a ruling
and an oppressed class, was the necessary consequence of the
deficient and restricted development of production in former
times. So long as the total social labour only yields a produce which but slightly exceeds that barely necessary for
the existence of all; so long, therefore, as labour engages all
or almost all the time of the great majority of the members
of society—so long, of necessity, this society is divided into
classes. Side by side with the great majority, exclusively
bond slaves to labour, arises a class freed from directly
productive labour, which looks after the general affairs of
society: the direction of labour, state business, law, science,
art, etc. It is, therefore, the law of division of labour that

lies at the basis of the division into classes. But this does not prevent this division into classes from being carried out by means of violence and robbery, trickery and fraud. It does not prevent the ruling class, once having the upper hand, from consolidating its power at the expense of the working class, from turning its social leadership into an intensified exploitation of the masses.

But if, upon this showing, division into classes has a certain historical justification, it has this only for a given period, only under given social conditions. It was based upon the insufficiency of production. It will be swept away by the complete development of modern productive forces. And, in fact, the abolition of classes in society presupposes a degree of historical evolution at which the existence, not simply of this or that particular ruling class, but of any ruling class at all, and, therefore, the existence of class distinction itself has become an obsolete anachronism. It presupposes, therefore, the development of production carried out to a degree at which appropriation of the means of production and of the products, and, with this, of political domination, of the monopoly of culture, and of intellectual leadership by a particular class of society, has become not only superfluous but economically, politically, and intellectually a hindrance to development.

This point is now reached. Their political and intellectual bankruptcy is scarcely any longer a secret to the bourgeoisie themselves. Their economic bankruptcy recurs regularly every ten years. In every crisis society is suffocated beneath the weight of its own productive forces and products, which it cannot use, and stands helpless, face to face with the absurd contradiction that the producers have nothing to consume because consumers are wanting. The expansive force of the means of production bursts the bonds that the capitalist mode of production had imposed upon them. Their deliverance from these bonds is the one precondition for an unbroken, constantly accelerated development of the productive forces, and therewith for a practically unlimited increase of production itself. Nor is this all. The socialised appropriation of the means of production does away not only with the present artificial restrictions upon production but also with the positive waste and devastation of productive forces and products that are at the present time the inevitable concomitants of production and that reach their height in the crises. Further, it sets free for the community at large a mass of means of production and of products by doing away with the senseless extravagance of the ruling classes of today and their political representatives. The possibility of securing for every member of society, by means of socialised production, an existence not only fully sufficient materially, and becoming day by day more full, but an existence guaranteeing to all the free development and exercise of their physical and mental faculties—this possibility is now for the first time here, but *it is here*.

With the seizing of the means of production by society, production of commodities is done away with, and, simultaneously, the mastery of the product over the producer. Anarchy in social production is replaced by systematic, definite organisation. The struggle for individual existence disappears. Then for the first time man, in a certain sense, is finally marked off from the rest of the animal kingdom, and emerges from mere animal conditions of existence into really human ones. The whole sphere of the conditions of life which environ man, and which have hitherto ruled man, now comes under the dominion and control of man, who for the first time becomes the real, conscious lord of nature, because he has now become master of his own social organisation. The laws of his own social action, hitherto standing face to face with man as laws of nature foreign to and dominating him, will then be used with full understanding, and so mastered by him. Man's own social organisation, hitherto confronting him as a necessity imposed by nature and history, now becomes the result of his own free action. The extraneous objective forces that have hitherto governed history pass under the control of man himself. Only from that time will man himself, more and more consciously, make his own history—only from that time will the social causes set in movement by him have, in the main and in a constantly growing measure, the results intended by him. It is the ascent of man from the kingdom of necessity to the kingdom of freedom.

2

The Catholic

IT IS a pernicious illusion to suppose that men can become
the lords of nature and masters of society and so liberate
themselves from all their ills. But in order to throw off that
illusion we must understand the relations that bind men
together into a society.

These relations are of different kinds. There are, for example, physical relations and economic relations: we catch
diseases from one another; we buy products and sell our
services. What is remarkable about relations of these kinds
is that they are not, directly, moral relations, involving our
intelligence and will. I can give you a disease or affect your
life through the market without being in the least conscious
that I am doing so. My behaviour can cause an epidemic,
or help to precipitate an economic crisis, while I remain
oblivious.

There are, however, relations of quite other kinds; for
example, moral relations, involving rights and duties. Here
consciousness is of the essence. There can be no relationship
of having a right to be treated or a duty to act in a certain
way unless the beings involved can recognise in some degree
the right or duty in question. Of all the factors that distinguish men from other terrestrial creatures none is more
important than this capacity to enter into, and determine
their behaviour by, a system of mutual obligations. To see
this we have only to consider how much time we spend
developing in our children, by precept, prohibition, and
example, their latent power to grasp moral rules in principle, to apply them in practice, and so in due course to
enter fully into the moral universe of man.

These plain truths have hardly ever been directly denied,
either in the practical affairs of society or in the views of

theoreticians. What has been denied, explicitly or implicitly, is the pre-eminent importance of moral relations
over all others. Society is human precisely to the extent that
the men and women who compose it are conscious of their
reciprocal rights and duties, seek to increase this consciousness in themselves and one another, work for a progressively
closer fellowship in this world of spiritual values, apply
themselves seriously to respecting others' rights and to dis-
charging their own obligations, and strive in every way to
subordinate all other types of relationship, such as the physical and the economic, to this moral order. Human society
is realised in freedom, in the lives, that is, of men and women
who take and accept responsibility for their actions precisely
because they are rational moral beings.

Seen from this point of view the time in which we live has
two outstanding characteristics.

The first of these is the vastly increased and ever more
rapidly increasing range of human activities with respect to
which the moral order can and must be asserted. Science and
industry, in giving men new powers, have also given them
new responsibilities. We now can and must solve the problems of poverty, inequality, war and injustice, both within
and between all the societies in which men are organised.
We can, because science has given us the knowledge and
economic progress the resources; we must, because otherwise
we shall destroy ourselves. We therefore live at a time of
supreme challenge. The moral order must be asserted over
all other forces in human life as never before if man is not to
put an end to himself and the values he embodies.

But if the first great mark of our time is the new responsibility of new power, the second is the terrible ignorance of
the true nature of that responsibility and of the conditions
under which it can be exercised. The truth is that the moral
order and the human freedom that goes with it are not
self-made, self-sufficient, and self-supporting. Men—moral,
rational men—have not made themselves; God made them;
and God made them not for themselves but for Himself.
Consequently their hearts can find no rest until they rest in
Him; consequently, however much scientific and economic
progress men may make there will be no peace or justice in
the world until they return to a sense of their dignity as the
creatures and sons of God, the first and final cause of all

created being. To try to enhance man's greatness independently of God, to try to restrain, even to eliminate, the
soul's upward surge towards God: that is both the most
striking and the most pernicious error of our time.

If, then, we are to shoulder the responsibility that knowledge and power have thrust upon us it is necessary that this
error should be clearly exposed and the truth clearly established.

Let us take the most crucial case, the case of war.

Although individuals and nations are becoming more and
more convinced of the necessity of international co-operation and understanding, it seems that men in general, and
politicians in particular, are incapable of achieving it. The
trouble is the lack of mutual trust. Men and states are in
mortal fear that others are harbouring and preparing plans
of conquest; hence each organises its own defence, squander-
ing, in consequence, vast human and natural resources;
hence a growing uneasiness gnaws at men's hearts and
makes them less responsive to the call of nobler enterprises.

The root cause of this deadly mistrust is the presence of
ideological differences between nations, and more especially
between their rulers. Both sides, for example, speak in terms
of 'justice', but the word takes on different meanings
according to which side is using it, so that the common use
of it only serves to intensify the impression that the other is
hatching sinister and selfish designs behind a hypocritical
display of disinterested virtue. This experience has even
brought people to the point of denying the existence of any
binding moral order. But where the same law of justice is
not both seen and kept, not only can men not hope to come
to open and full agreement on vital issues, but they end up
with the impression that the only way open to them is the
recourse to violence.

It follows that men can only escape from the present
danger of self-destruction by establishing a common law of
justice. How can this be done?

It is plain that it cannot be done so long as men consider
themselves exclusively as members of society, and, therefore, as members of some particular society or other. We
are in search—in urgent search—of a moral order, including
a law of justice, common to all men, at all times, everywhere. Social relations, on the other hand, are infinitely

various and changeful. It follows that the moral order can only be universally and absolutely binding if, in relation to societies, it is transcendent. However much it may be true that man is made for life in society and cannot exist outside society, it is also true that he is not exclusively, not even primarily, made for social life: he is made by God for God; he is therefore, as an individual, prior to society. That fact alone explains the moral order; and the recognition of it alone endows the moral order with its proper strength. For the moral order simply prescribes the conditions that men must observe in their conduct with each other for each to be to God as God requires. Thus the moral order has no existence except in God, and no strength except through faith in God. As applied to the particular problem of war: there can be no peace between men unless there is peace within each one of them: unless, that is, each one builds up within himself the order God requires. Only in our common position as the children of God can we find and accept that absolute and universal equality on which the moral order rests; only so can man find peace.

This essential point once grasped, all our difficulties become clear in principle, however complex—and various— their solutions may turn out to be in practice. The recognition of our equality before God not only provides us with the fixed point by holding on to which our ideological differences, and the sinister mistrust they breed, are to be overcome; it similarly provides us with the means to deal with all our social problems. Whether it is a question of redressing those imbalances of power between industries, regions, countries, and classes which lead to a grossly unjust distribution of wealth and opportunity; whether it is a question of reconsidering the role of property in modern societies in order to determine why and how far it is desirable as an essential expression and guarantee of individual freedom, and how far not; whether it is a question of understanding and defending the supreme importance of the family as being the social unit most nearly affecting the moral and religious destiny of the individual; whether even it is a question about the permissibility of such a particular practice as contraception: in every case the absolute priority of the relationship between each individual and his God, and the absolute equality of individuals before the God who made

them all, form the essential starting point for a true understanding of man's social situation, now as always.

So much can be known by natural reason, and is indeed
common not only to all Christians but also to adherents of
many other faiths; it is not, however, all that is essential to
salvation. For man to be saved it is necessary for him to
know not merely that God exists but that He exists as a
unity of three persons; that God the Father created the world,
and man within it, out of nothing; that He endowed man
with freedom of the will, which man then used to break
God's law; that to redeem mankind from this ancestral taint
the second Person of the Trinity, God the Son, became a
man, as Jesus Christ, and suffered death at human hands;
and that He instituted the Church as the perpetual vehicle
of the human salvation which He had begun, and of the
sacred truths which, following upon the Hebrew prophets,
He had revealed. For the truths that are most essential to
man's salvation—the truths, for example, about the person
and the work of Christ Himself—cannot be discovered by
unaided reason but can only be made known to those who
believe in Christ and in His Church.

It follows that in the development of that human understanding the Church has an essential role to play. For in so
far as the individual is left to his own resources, his relationship to his God is corrupted, and his understanding of that
relationship confused, by the sinfulness that is inherent in
him. By Christ, as God on earth, and by Christ alone, was the
conquest of sin made possible, and the relationship and understanding between man and God restored; by the Church,
as the representative of Christ, and by the Church alone, are
they maintained through time. Outside the Church there is
no salvation. Hence, the Church alone can fully understand
the true nature of that human equality before God upon
which social understanding rests; she is the Mother and
Teacher of all nations, the pillar and ground of truth. While
the Church's first care must be to sanctify souls and make
them share in the gifts of heaven, just because the power to
do that is her special privilege, she alone can fully understand the needs of man's daily life and lay down the principles by which it should be organised.

The laying down of these principles and their application
to concrete situations are, of course, difficult tasks, particu-

larly at a time when the concrete situation is constantly changing. Indeed, just because of this dynamism of human society, so much more evident now than ever before, the problem of bringing social reality into line with the objective requirements of justice is one that can never be definitively solved. In this connection two things should be noted. The first is that the natural laws of justice by which men's relations with each other should be regulated is in outline, if not in essence, comprehensible by reason independently of faith, so that the Church can to that extent co-operate with men of goodwill and understanding everywhere. The second is that the application of those natural laws demands expert knowledge that goes beyond the competence of the Church as such. It follows that while the laws of justice between men are absolute, and only fully illuminated when set in the light of faith, yet they can be apprehended by all sorts of men and must be applied by all sorts of institutions and professions. On this basis, relative solutions to the problem of justice are possible. To see what this means let us in conclusion consider two such problems: the problem of international order, which we have already raised, and the problem of life in industrial society.

We saw that a common acknowledgment of man's equality before God is the only basis on which men can allay the mistrust between nations. The truth is that mankind has always formed a spiritual unity; all that has happened during recent centuries is that human beings, already spiritually one, have been brought materially and practically together by commerce, communications, and many other practical influences. Does not every man of good sense and goodwill realise that the unity of men is something spiritual and absolute, transcending all their practical connections and giving them their true significance? This feeling is what the doctrine of the Church makes plain. Now the crucial fact of our time is that the national, sovereign state is no longer sufficient to tackle the problems before us. The moral order, which needs public authorities in order to promote the common good, also requires that these authorities should be effective; but the community of independent sovereign states cannot be effective in solving, for example, the problems posed by nuclear power. In these circumstances it is tempting to look for the solution in a worldwide public authority, imposed by the force of the more powerful political communities. But precisely there can we see the true significance and strength of the Church's doctrine of human equality and justice. For the world political authority must not only be effective; it must be impartial; and if it is not impartial it will not be effective, given the great sensitivity of states as regards their juridical equality and moral dignity. But how can it be impartial if it is not set up by the voluntary consent of all states? We thus see not merely that the problems of peace can only be solved on the basis of the equality of men before God, but that the acceptance of that equality requires, in present circumstances, the transcendence of the sovereign state not by some new kind of empire but by an act of free association.

War, however, although the most obvious, is not the only way in which man is in danger of forgetting his true nature and destroying himself. Modern man has vastly increased his understanding and control of nature. His achievements to date deserve ungrudging admiration, and there are more to come. Nevertheless, this striving to master and transform the world around him has its evils and dangers: it corrupts both work and leisure. Work, which was decreed by Providence for the good of man, often changes in the factory into an instrument of perversion, so that while dead matter goes out improved, the worker is degraded by the monotony and irresponsibility of his job. He then sees the rest of life as the mere quest for pleasure and the satisfaction of human passions. These two factors work upon each other and are disastrous in their effects, undermining as they do the autonomy, and therefore the true dignity, of the individual, both in relation to his fellows and in relation to his lower inclinations. Man is thus making himself a giant in the physical world at the expense of his spirit, which is reduced to a pygmy in the supernatural and eternal world.

The remedy for these evils lies in rejecting absolutely the doctrine that man's true greatness consists first and foremost in the mastery of nature and then in working out the consequences of that rejection in a new set of social principles. What is wanted is a new charter of rights and duties which does as full justice to the spiritual as to the material needs of man. The list of these rights and duties must, of course, be long; but of particular importance is the right of the worker to have a say in the affairs of the firm in which he works and the duty of employers to make that possible by new forms of organised participation. Any kind of organisation which diminishes the responsibility of the individual is to that extent bad; every step must be taken to increase it in industrial as in political and family life.

To conclude: man, because he is corrupted by inherent sin, can only be truly liberated by God, that is by Christ, that is by the Church as the representative of Christ. True liberation is the salvation of the soul from sin. But, since men live together in society, the forms in which they do so can, to a greater or lesser extent, promote that liberation of their souls from sin, which, left to themselves, they are unable to achieve. It is therefore the right and duty of the Church, acting on behalf of mankind, to keep a constant, critical eye upon the forms of social life, separating those which are favourable to salvation from those which are unfavourable, and explaining how the true spiritual freedom of man can be supported by particular terrestrial freedoms appropriate to the times. Typical of such freedoms in our times are that of the worker to participate in the control of industry and of men everywhere to control their destinies by a more effective political organisation than the independent sovereign state. But, important as such freedoms are, we must always remember that they are secondary, both in their nature and in the means by which they are to be attained. Men must seek first the kingdom of God; then, and only then, will all these things be added unto them; then and only then will they know a freedom that is eternal and entire.

3

The Democrat

JEFFERSON

WE hold these truths to be self-evident:
    that all men are created equal;
    that they are endowed by their Creator with certain unalienable rights;
    that among these are life, liberty, and the pursuit of happiness;
    that to secure these rights, governments are instituted among men, deriving their just powers from the consent of the governed;
    that whenever any form of government becomes destructive of these ends it is the right of the people to alter or to abolish it, and to institute new government, laying its foundation on such principles and organising its powers in such form as to them shall seem most likely to effect their safety and happiness.

I have sworn upon the altar of God eternal hostility against every form of tyranny over the mind of man.

All eyes are opened, or opening, to the rights of man. The general spread of the light of science has already laid open to every view the palpable truth, that the mass of mankind has not been born with saddles on their backs, nor a favoured few booted and spurred, ready to ride them legitimately, by the grace of God.

I believe . . . that morality, compassion, generosity, are
innate elements of the human constitution; that there exists
a right independent of force; that a right to property is
founded in our natural wants, in the means with which we
are endowed to satisfy these wants, and the right to what we
acquire by those means without violating the similar rights
of other sensible beings; that no one has a right to obstruct
another, exercising his faculties innocently for the relief of
sensibilities made a part of his nature; that justice is the
fundamental law of society; that the majority, oppressing
an individual, is guilty of a crime, abuses its strength, and,
by acting on the law of the strongest, breaks up the foundations of society; that action by the citizens in person, in
affairs within their reach and competence, and in all others
by representatives, chosen immediately, and removable by
themselves, constitutes the essence of a republic; that all
governments are more or less republican in proportion as
this principle enters more or less into their composition; and
that a government by representation is capable of extension
over a greater surface of country than one of any other form.

In every government on earth is some trace of human
weakness, some germ of corruption and degeneracy, which
cunning will discover, and wickedness insensibly open, culti-
vate, and improve. Every government degenerates when
trusted to the rulers of the people alone. The people themselves are its only safe depositories. And to render even them
safe their minds must be improved to a certain degree . . .
An amendment of our constitution must here come in aid of
the public education. The influence over government must
be shared among all the people. If every individual . . . par-
ticipates of the ultimate authority, the government will be
safe.

If a nation expects to be ignorant and free, in a state of
civilisation, it expects what never was and never will be. The
functionaries of every government have propensities to command at will the liberty and property of their constituents
There is no safe deposit for these but with the people themselves; nor can they be safe with them without information.

Where the Press is free, and every man able to read, all is safe.

In every country where man is free to think, and to speak, differences of opinion will arise from difference of perception and the imperfection of reason; but these differences, when permitted, as in this happy country, to purify themselves by free discussion, are but as passing clouds overspreading our land transiently, and leaving our horizon more bright and serene. That love of order and obedience to the laws, which so remarkably characterise the citizens of the United States, are sure pledges of internal tranquillity; and the elective franchise, if guarded as the act of our safety, will peaceably dissipate all combinations to subvert a Constitution dictated by the wisdom and resting on the will of the people. That will is the only legitimate foundation of any government.

Trial by jury, I consider as the only anchor ever yet imagined by man, by which a government can be held to the principles of its constitution.

No person living wishes more sincerely than I do to see a complete refutation of the doubts I have myself entertained and expressed on the grade of understanding allotted to them [Negroes] by nature, and to find that in this respect they are on a par with ourselves. My doubts were the result of personal observation in the limited sphere of my own State, where the opportunities for the development of their genius were not favourable, and those of exercising it still less so. . . . But whatever be their degree of talent it is no measure of their rights. Because Sir Isaac Newton was superior to others in understanding he was not therefore lord of the person or property of others.

The whole commerce between master and slave is a perpetual exercise of the most boisterous passions, the most unremitting despotism on the one part, and degrading submissions on the other. The man must be a prodigy who can retain his manners and morals undepraved by such circumstances.

LINCOLN

I have never had a feeling politically that did not spring from the sentiments embodied in the Declaration of Independence. I have often pondered over the dangers which were incurred by the men who adopted that Declaration of Independence —I have pondered over the toils that were endured by the officers and soldiers of the army, who achieved that independence. I have often enquired of myself what great principle or idea it was that kept this Confederacy so long together. It was not the mere matter of the separation of the colonies from the motherland; but something in that Declaration giving liberty not alone to the people of this country, but hope to the world for all future time. It was that which gave promise that in due time the weights should be lifted from the shoulders of all men, and that *all* should have an equal chance. This is the sentiment embodied in that Declaration of Independence.

Our Declaration of Independence says:
'We hold these truths to be self-evident: that all men are created equal; that they are endowed by their Creator with certain inalienable rights; that among these are life, liberty, and the pursuit of happiness. That to secure these rights, governments are instituted among men, DERIVING THEIR JUST POWERS FROM THE CONSENT OF THE GOVERNED.'

I have quoted so much at this time merely to show that according to our ancient faith the just powers of governments are derived from the consent of the governed. Now the relation of masters and slaves is, *pro tanto*, a total violation of this principle. The master not only governs the slave without his consent; but he governs him by a set of rules altogether different from those which he prescribes for himself. Allow *all* the governed an equal voice in the government, and that, and that only, is self-government. . . .

Our government rests in public opinion. Whoever can

change public opinion can change the government, practically just so much. Public opinion, on any subject, always has a *central idea*, from which all its minor thoughts radiate. That 'central idea' in our political public opinion at the beginning was, and until recently has continued to be, 'the equality of men'. And although it was always submitted patiently to whatever of inequality there seemed to be as matter of actual necessity, its constant working has been a steady progress towards the practical equality of all men. The late presidential election was a struggle, by one party, to discard that central idea, and to substitute for it the opposite idea that slavery is right, in the abstract, the workings of which, as a central idea, may be the perpetuity of human slavery, and its extension to all countries and colours.

Our progress in degeneracy appears to me to be pretty rapid. As a nation we began by declaring that *'all men are created equal'*. We now practically read it 'all men are created equal, *except Negroes'*. When the Know-Nothings get control it will read 'all men are created equal, except Negroes, *and foreigners and catholics'*. When it comes to this I should prefer emigrating to some country where they make no pretence of loving liberty—to Russia, for instance, where despotism can be taken pure, and without the base alloy of hypocrisy.

We have besides these men—descended by blood from our ancestors—among us perhaps half our people who are not descendants at all of these men; they are men who have come from Europe—German, Irish, French, and Scandinavian—men that have come from Europe themselves, or whose ancestors have come hither and settled here, finding themselves our equals in all things. If they look back through this history to trace their connection with those days by blood they find they have none, they cannot carry themselves back into that glorious epoch and make themselves feel that they are part of us, but when they look through that old Declaration of Independence they find that those old men say that 'We hold these truths to be self-evident, that all men are created equal', and then they feel that that moral sentiment taught in that day evidences their relation to those men, that it is the father of all moral principle in them, and that they have a right to claim it as though they were blood of the blood and flesh of the flesh of the men who wrote that Declaration, and so they are. That is the electric cord in that Declaration that links the hearts of patriotic and liberty-loving men together, that will link those patriotic hearts as long as the love of freedom exists in the minds of men throughout the world.

Four score and seven years ago our fathers brought forth on this continent a new nation, conceived in Liberty; and dedicated to the proposition that all men are created equal.

Now we are engaged in a great civil war, testing whether that nation, or any nation so conceived and so dedicated, can long endure. We are met on a great battlefield of that war. We have come to dedicate a portion of that field as a final resting place for those who here gave their lives that that nation might live. It is altogether fitting and proper that we should do this.

But, in a larger sense, we cannot dedicate—we cannot consecrate—we cannot hallow—this ground. The brave men, living and dead, who struggled here have consecrated it far above our poor power to add or detract. The world will little note, nor long remember what we say here, but it can never forget what they did here. It is for us the living, rather, to be dedicated here to the unfinished work which they who fought here have thus far so nobly advanced. It is rather for us to be here dedicated to the great task remaining before us—that from these honoured dead we take increased devotion to that cause for which they gave the last full measure of devotion —that we here highly resolve that these dead shall not have died in vain—that this nation, under God, shall have a new birth of freedom—and that government of the people, by the people, for the people, shall not perish from the earth.

WILSON

I don't care how benevolent the master is going to be. I will not live under a master. That is not what America was created for. America was created in order that every man should have the same chance with every other man to exercise mastery over his own fortunes.

You know what the processes of modern society are. They are not individualistic. They are processes of association, and those processes contain in them a danger that governments never saw before. Because men never before had the means or the genius for association that they have now, and the danger at the present moment is that private association will become stronger than public association, and that there will be combinations of men and of money stronger than the government itself. If we take this thing in hand now it may be that we shall prevail. If we do not take it in hand now it may be that we shall not prevail. The time is all too long postponed. The danger is so great that it will need all the prudence, all the moderation, all the intelligence, all the good nature of America, to revive her ancient standards and re-practise her ancient principles.

Why, government was set up in America because men of all classes were not served anywhere else in the world! Under every other government in the world, when American government was set up, the government served only some of the classes of the community, and we boasted, we hoped, we were confident that we had set up a government in this country which would serve every class without discrimination—the most humble along with the most powerful. Only so long as we keep American government up to that ideal and standard will it be worthy of the name America.

I believe that the greatest force for peace, the greatest force for righteousness, the greatest force for the elevation of mankind, is organised opinion, is the thinking of men, is the great force which is in the soul of men, and I want men to breathe a free and pure air.

Ladies and gentlemen, what are the liberties of a people? I have often had an image of liberty in my mind, an illustration of it. You know that when a great engine runs free, as we say, its freedom consists in its perfect adjustment. All the parts are so assembled and united and accommodated that there is no friction but a united power in all the parts. So I dream of political liberty when we understand one another, when we co-operate with one another. When we are united with one another, then we are free. And when the American people have thus joined together in the great enterprise of their common life they will wonder how it ever happened that they permitted the great special interests to grow up and overshadow the wholesome growths of the garden; then they shall wonder that it was ever necessary to summon them to the conclusions of the ballot. I propose that men now forget their individual likes and dislikes, their individual sympathies and antipathies, and, drawing together in the solemn act of a sovereign people, determine what the government of the United States shall be.

What I am interested in is having the government of the United States more concerned about human rights than about property rights. Property is an instrument of humanity. Humanity isn't an instrument of property. And yet when you see some men engaged in some kinds of industries riding their great industries as if they were driving a car or juggernaut, not looking to see what multitudes prostrate themselves before the car and lose their lives in the crushing effect of their industry, you wonder how long men are going to be permitted to think more of their machinery than they think of their men. Did you never think of it? Men are cheap and machinery is dear, and many a superintendent will be dismissed for overdriving a delicate machine who wouldn't be dismissed for overdriving an overtaxed man. Because you can discard one man and replace him; there are others ready to come into his place; but you can't without great cost discard your machine and put a new one in its place. You are not looking upon your men as the essential and vital foundation part of your whole business. I say, therefore, that property as compared with humanity, as compared with the vital red blood in the American people, must take second place, not first place; and that we must see to it that there is no overcrowding, that there is no bad sanitation, that there is no unnecessary spread of avoidable diseases, that there is every safeguard against accidents, that women are not driven to impossible tasks and children not permitted to spend their energy before it is fit to be spent, that all the hope of the race must be preserved, and that men must be preserved according to their individual needs and not according to the programme of industry merely. Because, what is the use having industry if we die in producing it? If we die in trying to get a foothold in the crowd, why not let the crowd trample us sooner and be done with it? I tell you, gentlemen, that there is beginning to beat in this nation a great pulse of irresistible sympathy which is going to transform the process of government amongst us.

ROOSEVELT

Four hundred years ago, in Europe as well as in Asia, there was little hope of liberty for the average men of courage and goodwill. The ambitions of a ruling class and the times alike conspired against liberty of conscience, liberty of speech, liberty of the person, liberty of economic opportunity. Wars, dynastic and religious, had exhausted both the substance and the tolerance of the Old World. There was neither economic nor political liberty—nor any hope for either.

Then came one of the great ironies of history. Rulers needed to find gold to pay their armies and increase their power over the common men. The seamen they sent to find that gold found instead the way of escape for the common man from those rulers. What they found over the Western horizon was not the silk and jewels of Cathay but mankind's second chance—a chance to create a new world after he had almost spoiled the old one.

And the Almighty seems purposefully to have withheld that second chance until the time when men would most need and appreciate liberty, the time when men would be enlightened enough to establish it on foundations sound enough to maintain it.

For over three centuries a steady stream of men, women, and children followed the beacon of liberty which this light symbolises. They brought to us strength and moral fibre developed in a civilisation centuries old but fired anew by the dream of a better life in America. They brought to one new country the cultures of a hundred old ones. . . . They adopted this homeland because in this land they found a home in which the things they most desired could be theirs —freedom of opportunity, freedom of thought, freedom to worship God. Here they found life because here was freedom to live.

I see a great nation, upon a great continent, blessed with a great wealth of natural resources. Its hundred and thirty million people are at peace among themselves; they are making their country a good neighbour among the nations. I see a United States which can demonstrate that, under democratic methods of government, national wealth can be translated into a spreading volume of human comforts hitherto unknown, and the lowest standard of living can be raised far above the level of mere subsistence.

But here is the challenge to our democracy: In this nation I see tens of millions of its citizens—a substantial part of its whole population—who at this very moment are denied the greater part of what the very lowest standards of today call the necessities of life.

It is not in despair that I paint you that picture. I paint it for you in hope—because the nation, seeing and understanding the injustice in it, proposes to paint it out. We are determined to make every American citizen the subject of his country's interest and concern; and we will never regard any faithful, law-abiding group within our borders as superfluous. The test of our progress is not whether we add more to the abundance of those who have much; it is whether we provide enough for those who have too little.

If I know aught of the spirit and purpose of our nation we will not listen to Comfort, Opportunism, and Timidity. We will carry on.

Overwhelmingly, we of the Republic are men and women of goodwill; men and women who have more than warm hearts of dedication; men and women who have cool heads and willing hands of practical purpose as well. They will insist that every agency of popular government use effective instruments to carry out their will.

When four years ago we met to inaugurate a President, the Republic, single-minded in anxiety, stood in spirit here. We dedicated ourselves to the fulfilment of a vision—to speed the time when there would be for all the people that security and peace essential to the pursuit of happiness. We of the Republic pledged ourselves to drive from the temple of our ancient faith those who had profaned it; to end by action, tireless and unafraid, the stagnation and despair of that day. We did those first things first.

Our covenant with ourselves did not stop there. Instinctively we recognised a deeper need—the need to find through government the instrument of our united purpose to solve for the individual the ever-rising problems of a complex civilisation. Repeated attempts at their solution without the aid of government had left us baffled and bewildered. For, without that aid, we had been unable to create those moral controls over the services of science which are necessary to make science a useful servant instead of a ruthless master of mankind. To do this we knew that we must find practical controls over blind economic forces and blindly selfish men.

We of the Republic sensed the truth that democratic government has innate capacity to protect its people against disasters once considered inevitable, to solve problems once considered unsolvable. We would not admit that we could not find a way to master economic epidemics, just as, after centuries of fatalistic suffering, we had found a way to master epidemics of disease. We refused to leave the problems of our common welfare to be solved by the winds of chance and the hurricanes of disaster.

In this we Americans were discovering no wholly new truth; we were writing a new chapter in our book of self-government.

KENNEDY

We observe today not a victory of party but a celebration of freedom, symbolising an end as well as a beginning, signifying renewal as well as change. For I have sworn before you and Almighty God the same solemn oath our forbears prescribed nearly a century and three-quarters ago.

The world is very different now. For man holds in his mortal hands the power to abolish all forms of human poverty and all forms of human life. And yet the same revolutionary belief for which our forbears fought is still at issue around the globe, the belief that the rights of man come not from the generosity of the state but from the hand of God.

We dare not forget today that we are the heirs of that first revolution. Let the word go forth from this time and place, to friend and foe alike, that the torch has been passed to a new generation of Americans, born in this century, tempered by war, disciplined by a hard and bitter peace, proud of our ancient heritage, and unwilling to witness or permit the slow undoing of those human rights to which this nation has always been committed, and to which we are committed today at home and around the world.

Let every nation know, whether it wishes us well or ill, that we shall pay any price, bear any burden, meet any hardship, support any friend, oppose any foe to assure the survival and the success of liberty.

This much we pledge—and more.

To those old allies whose cultural and spiritual origins we share, we pledge the loyalty of faithful friends. United, there is little we cannot do in a host of co-operative ventures. Divided, there is little we can do, for we dare not meet a powerful challenger at odds and split asunder.

To those new states whom we welcome to the ranks of the free we pledge our word that one form of colonial control shall not have passed away merely to be replaced by a far more iron tyranny. We shall not always expect to find them supporting our view. But we shall always hope to find them strongly supporting their own freedom, and to remember that, in the past, those who foolishly sought power by riding the back of the tiger ended up inside.

To those people in the huts and villages of half the globe struggling to break the bonds of mass misery we pledge our best efforts to help them help themselves, for whatever period is required, not because the Communists may be doing it, not because we seek their votes, but because it is

right. If a free society cannot help the many who are poor it cannot save the few who are rich.

To our sister republics south of our border we offer a special pledge: to convert our good words into good deeds, in a new alliance for progress, to assist free men and free governments in casting off the chains of poverty. But this peaceful revolution of hope cannot become the prey of hostile powers. Let all our neighbours know that we shall join with them to oppose aggression or subversion anywhere in the Americas. And let every other power know that this hemisphere intends to remain master of its own house.

To that world assembly of sovereign states, the United Nations, our last best hope in an age where the instruments of war have far outpaced the instruments of peace, we renew our pledge of support: to prevent it from becoming merely a forum for invective, to strengthen its shield of the new and the weak, and to enlarge the area in which its writ may run.

Finally, to those nations who would make themselves our adversary, we offer not a pledge but a request: that both sides begin anew the quest for peace, before the dark powers of destruction unleashed by science engulf all humanity in planned or accidental self-destruction.

We dare not tempt them with weakness. For only when our arms are sufficient beyond doubt can we be certain beyond doubt that they will never be employed.

But neither can two great and powerful groups of nations take comfort from our present course—both sides overburdened by the cost of modern weapons, both rightly alarmed by the steady spread of the deadly atom, yet both racing to alter that uncertain balance of terror that stays the hand of mankind's final war.

So let us begin anew, remembering on both sides that civility is not a sign of weakness, and sincerity is always subject to proof. Let us never negotiate out of fear, but let us never fear to negotiate.

Let both sides explore what problems unite us instead of belabouring those problems which divide us.

Let both sides, for the first time, formulate serious and precise proposals for the inspection and control of arms, and bring the absolute power to destroy other nations under the absolute control of all nations.

Let both sides seek to invoke the wonders of science instead of its terrors. Together let us explore the stars, conquer the deserts, eradicate disease, tap the ocean depths, and encourage the arts and commerce.

Let both sides unite to heed in all corners of the earth the command of Isaiah to 'undo the heavy burdens . . . (and) let the oppressed go free'.

And if a beach-head of co-operation may push back the jungle of suspicion let both sides join in creating a new endeavour, not a new balance of power, but a new world of law, where the strong are just and the weak secure and the peace preserved.

All this will not be finished in the first one hundred days. Nor will it be finished in the first one thousand days, nor in the life of this Administration, nor even perhaps in our lifetimes on this planet. But let us begin.

In your hands, my fellow-citizens, more than mine, will rest the final success or failure of our course. Since this country was founded, each generation of Americans has been summoned to give testimony to its national loyalty. The graves of young Americans who answered the call to service surround the globe.

Now the trumpet summons us again—not as a call to bear arms, though arms we need; not as a call to battle, though embattled we are; but a call to bear the burden of a long twilight struggle, year in and year out, rejoicing in hope, patient in tribulation', a struggle against the common enemies of man : tyranny, poverty, disease, and war itself.

Can we forge against these enemies a grand and global alliance, North and South, East and West, that can assure a more fruitful life for all mankind? Will you join in that historic effort?

In the long history of the world only a few generations have been granted the role of defending freedom in its hour of maximum danger. I do not shrink from this responsibility; I welcome it. I do not believe that any of us would exchange places with any other people or any other generation. The energy, the faith, the devotion which we bring to this endeavour will light our country and all who serve it, and the glow from that fire can truly light the world.

And so, my fellow-Americans, ask not what your country can do for you; ask what you can do for your country.

My fellow-citizens of the world, ask not what America will

do for you, but what together we can do for the freedom of man.

Finally, whether you are citizens of America or citizens of the world, ask of us here the same high standards of strength and sacrifice which we ask of you. With a good conscience our only sure reward, with history the final judge of our deeds, let us go forth to lead the land we love, asking His blessing and His help, but knowing that here on earth God's work must truly be our own.

Second Remarks:
Ideology under Suspicion

THE first thing to be said about the ideologies that have just been expounded to us is that there are only three of them amongst the hundreds—or is it thousands?—that are active in the world today, let alone at earlier times; moreover, they cannot even be relied upon as being representative of the class as a whole. For example, they are all universal in their appeal; none of them are specifically restricted—as tribal myths and Judaism are—to a given race. Again, they all have strong implications for the reorganisation of society, and do not confine themselves—as Stoicism, Zen Buddhism, and evangelical Christianity tend to do—to the moral reform of individuals, taken by themselves. Indeed, they were chosen precisely because we live in the age of the political unification of mankind, to which they are particularly relevant. However, just because the three ideologies share those special features, we must be careful in drawing conclusions from them about ideologies in general.

The second thing to be said about these ideologies is that we shall get a false impression of them if we take them out of the whole situation of which they form a part. No examples can convey the most striking fact about modern ideologies: the immense amount of ideological activity that goes on around us. Books, articles, programmes, and speeches in their thousands and millions are devoted to ideological work by those three parties alone. And this vast quantity of material does not keep to the sober level of the examples. Most of it is concerned with the application of such general principles to particular situations, and with attacking the other side. Every aspect of human life, every move of the opponent, is watched, studied, and disputed. It would be a full-time job to keep abreast of the output of the ideologists of the two parts of Germany alone, as they defend their own *position and attack the other's in the minds of the German people. The examples must always therefore be thought of as multiplied a thousand times in volume and detail and vituperation. So multiplied, they would sound even more impressive than they do when standing on their own: but should we really be impressed? To answer that question we must compare what the ideologists purport to do with what they actually achieve.*

'The issue before us,' says the Marxist, 'is that of the liberation of man'; and with that his fellow-ideologists agree. They all set before us the goal of freedom and tell us how to reach it. And what, it may be said, could be more reasonable than that? Is not freedom a goal of great importance to us all? Are we not rational beings, who can work out ways of getting what we need? Should we not therefore work out how to get freedom?

But here is a disquieting comparison. Doctors also set before us a goal, health, and tell us how to reach it. That enterprise is eminently reasonable. There is general agreement about what health is, or at least about what is to be counted illness; in this field we know what is wanted. There is also general agreement as to the cause and cure of many illnesses; the doctors can often tell us how to be healthy. And while there are also many illnesses whose nature and treatment are still uncertain, doctors know how in principle to set about discovering both; medicine is a science. We can agree that it is reasonable to listen to doctors because, while they are sometimes mistaken and unhelpful, much more often they do not just tell us impressively what we should do to reach our aim of health, but prove in practice that they are right.

Now freedom, to which the ideologists profess to help us, may seem to be as definite a goal as health. Do we not all know what lack of freedom, as we knew what illness, is? But when we study what the ideologists have to say we find that there is little or no agreement on this point. Freedom, says the Marxist, consists in the mastery of nature and society; religion is slavery to human weakness. Freedom, says the Catholic, consists in obedience to God; mastery of the world is slavery to man's assertive pride. It is as if two doctors could not agree as to what is to be counted as an illness. And even when two ideologists do agree on the goal to be achieved they usually fail to agree on how to achieve it.

Russian and Chinese Marxists both look forward to the class-less society, Catholics and Protestants to the kingdom of heaven; but what is regarded by one as an essential step in those directions is regarded by his fellow as a fatal error. Now doctors, it is admitted, often disagree about the road to health; but while their disagreements can be, and daily are, cleared up by the agreed procedures of scientific method, the disagreements of the ideologists remain categorical and obdurate.

It is therefore not a carping, petty scepticism that forces us to doubt the ideologist's claims, but the claims themselves: the vagueness of their content and weakness of their argumentation.

And this is not the end of the matter. To scepticism about the ideologist's logic we can hardly avoid adding cynicism about his motives. It will escape no one but the simplest devotee that ideologies serve the interests of certain institutions, and therefore of those who hold office in those institutions. Men enjoy power, and the fruits of power. They like to make other men act as they decide; the spectacle is pleasant in itself and brings material gains. But how can other men be made obedient? It is impractical to be always telling and forcing them to act as you desire. That takes too much time; it is also too rigid, and is liable to produce resistance. More effective is to persuade them that obedience is in their own real interest; more effective still is to persuade them that what looks like obedience is really nothing of the kind, but rather the fulfilment of some plan or necessity which transcends the lives and needs of any individuals. (That the plan or necessity in question ministers much more to the lives and needs of some people than it does to those of others is merely incidental, and to be accepted as part of the nature of things.) These lines of thought thus lead to the conclusion that the social function of ideologies is to condition men intellectually to obedience. Condition men to believe that purity or self-control are the only things that matter, or that they are all equal because they have the vote, or that the Pope is the Vicar of God, or that the Party is the vehicle of Historical Necessity, and they will put up with an amazing amount of domination. And if anyone thinks this conclusion mischievous let him consider coolly who precisely makes ideological pronouncements and who precisely stands to gain by their being made. Is it the ordinary man? When this question is squarely faced the motives of the ideologist appear to be as suspect as his logic.

That does not mean that every ideologist is to be suspected of being, individually, a hypocrite. No doubt he often is; but he may just as often be the first to be beguiled by his own inventions. It means rather that while he claims that his theories are just as much based on reason as are those of a doctor, they are really irrational, and based on nothing more universal than the interests of parties and individuals. And while it is no more wrong for a man to work for his interests ideologically than it is wrong for him to work for them in any other way, it is wrong, in the sense of irrational, for another man to be taken in by the performance.

Ideology is therefore under suspicion: not merely in my mind, or for the sake of the argument of this book, but in your mind, and in the world at large. Whoever you are, and however strong your convictions, if you will take up this challenge in all truth and candour, and attend coolly to your feelings, you will I think discover—do you not?—at least a twinge of that suspicion; you will probably discover a great deal more. As for the world at large, if you will listen— coolly again—to the way in which most people respond to the pronouncements of their religious and political 'leaders', I have little doubt that you will find that your suspicion is widely shared. The way they talk about the nature and destiny of man strikes almost everyone as somewhat bogus; at least, it strikes so many people in that way that the doubt is not to be neglected.

Given this general scepticism about ideologies, how is an investigation of them to proceed? The best course, I think, will be to give our doubts free rein by handing the argument over to a full-blooded sceptic—part real, part imaginary— who will bring them together, work them out and put them over, without reserves. If we then find that we agree with him, well and good, we shall have reached our goal; if not, we shall at least know better where we stand, and what are the next steps to take.

So, having heard some ideologists making their own case and flaying one another's, let us listen for the next five chapters to a voice that, with impartial logic, flays them all.

PART TWO

THE
SCEPTIC
ATTACKS

4

Ideas as Weapons

IT IS curious to compare the methods of persuasion used by ideologists with those to be found in more modest fields of human endeavour.

A recent British advertisement for a brand of tea consisted of a picture of a canister with the name of the brand upon it and underneath the caption 'Free to Newlyweds'. Then followed not a word about the tea or its merits, but only instructions as to how any couple married between certain dates could obtain such a canister without payment. This advertisement, it appears, was highly successful; it introduced the tea to many people who were not newly married. As one of those responsible for devising it is said to have observed, you can sell anything with 'free'. Why so?

The mere use of the word 'free' is provocative and exciting. One has only to hear or to utter it for the air to clear, the pulse to quicken. One half fancies oneself striding out into the open or taking possession of things long desired. Add the word 'newlyweds' and the effect is multiplied; all sorts of agreeable things that have little to do with tea are free to newlyweds that were not free to them before, things just as tantalising to those who have known them as to those who have not. So, while ostensibly only offering a quarter of a pound of tea without payment, what the advertisement also did was to attach those latent longings to a brand of tea in such a way that when the brand was seen the longings were activated, and when the longings stirred the tea came to mind. As the longings are permanent, strong, and pleasant, sales of the brand then boom. But while the merits of the tea may then have their effect in persuading the buyer to buy more, neither they nor any argument for them have anything to do with the boom itself; this, in so far as it depended on purchases by people who were not newly married, was produced by exploiting the emotive properties of the word 'free' and the association of ideas. Canister, newlyweds, freedom: join them together and the job is done.

Such uses of the term are not limited to commerce. In a recent British election one of a series of Conservative posters depicted a dashing young couple picnicking in the country beside a sports car. The scene was attractive; the caption, as in others of the series, was just 'Conservative Freedom Works'. Now Conservative freedom—in Britain, at the present time—means freedom for the owners and controllers of capital to make what use of it they please with a minimum of political control; and while it is no doubt true that this freedom brings general advantages with it, and indeed that it brings to a small minority some of the advantages suggested by the picture—the sports car, for example—yet for the great majority of the population those advantages certainly do not extend to the enjoyment of romantic picnics. What, then, was the point of the poster? Why should it win votes?

In this example the glamorous picture played the part of the word 'newlywed' in the example of the tea. It tickled the imagination. The word 'freedom' brought with it its usual stimulation. The picture and word together gave the feeling of having and enjoying such a life. So young, so gay, so romantic! But 'freedom' was connected with the other words of the caption, as well as with the picture, with the result that that desirable existence was linked to the political economy of conservatism. Thus while the merits of Conservative economic policy may be great, to the power of this poster they were virtually irrelevant. This power resided in the linkage of the Conservative Party with gracious living by means of the flexible significance and emotive force of 'freedom'. The word can sell parties and policies as well as tea.

These examples make two points plain. First, 'freedom' and its cognates tend to convey directly both an emotion of excitement and some kind of favourable attitude to the thing or situation to which they are applied; second, while the emotion or the attitude that the word conveys normally have some connection with the objective properties of the thing in question, they need not do so. When a man released from prison describes himself as being free he expresses amongst other things his delight at being able to go where he pleases, a delight that will be shared by sympathetic spectators. The situation calls those favourable feelings forth, independently of anything that may be said about it. Consequently, the use of the word 'free' to describe it is perfectly clear and proper; a word whose normal function is to convey feelings is used of a situation in which those feelings exist, or are there to be evoked; the meaning of 'free' corresponds accurately to the objective features of the situation. But in the case of the tea the favourable attitude towards the thing had absolutely nothing to do with its own features; it was induced by a chain of associations depending on causal properties of the word itself. What, then, are those properties, and how does the word come to have them?

Emotions and attitudes are different things. Examples of emotions are fear, agitation, grief, joy; of attitudes, liking, hostility, affection, jealousy. Emotions involve an immediate disturbance of sensibility; those who have them are directly aware of them, while other people can only infer their existence from such involuntary reactions as blushing, pallor, the tempo of actions, and the pitch of voice; they normally arise from situations of which the subject is aware, but need not do so. Thus fear and joy simply feel different from each other; and while I am normally afraid of something that threatens me and joyful on account of some good fortune, these conditions can exist without my knowing why. I am sometimes inexplicably fearful, and on some days, objectively just like others, I am as inexplicably joyful from the moment I wake up. Attitudes, by contrast, imply the existence of an object towards which they are directed; they reveal themselves by complicated patterns of purposive behaviour in connection with the object in question; they are as plain or plainer to the observer as to the subject; and while immediate disturbances of sensibility usually go along with them, no such disturbance need take place at all. If I am hostile, I am hostile to something; I will tend, for instance, to avoid it, vote against it, or speak unfavourably of it, all of which will be at least as obvious to other parties as to myself; and though the presence or mention of this thing may make me angry on occasion, I am no less hostile towards it when I am not thinking of it at all or thinking of it with a cool resolution to do it down. Emotions and attitudes being so defined, the causal properties of the word 'freedom' with which we are dealing in these examples are those that it has of directly evoking emotion or excitement in the hearer and of inducing in him some kind of favourable atitude, such as liking, or support, for the object with which it happens to be associated. That the word has got these emotive and persuasive powers is put beyond doubt by the examples; but how does this come about, and what is its significance for thinking about freedom?

How 'freedom' gets these causal properties becomes clear with the elucidation of its logical force. The word has become emotive and persuasive by being used in certain circumstances, and it is the logical analysis of the meaning of the word that will establish what those circumstances are. To put the matter roughly for a start: when we think of freedom we think of people, especially ourselves, as no longer being thwarted by contrary circumstances; we think, for instance, of a man released from prison. Now we feel very strongly about being thwarted and about overcoming or avoiding the things that thwart us; strong emotions and strong attitudes are both involved. Hence, since these feelings arise normally out of the situations with respect to which we use the word, they get associated with the word itself. But once they have got associated with the word itself, an adroit use of the word will evoke the feelings dirctly and transfer them to an object which, like the tea, would not by itself call them forth at all. And the significance of this fact for thinking about freedom is that this mechanism can, as in the case of the tea, completely replace any rational thought about the qualities of an object, or, as in the political case, run parallel with what little rational thought there is and give it a practical force out of all proportion to its rational merits.

But to take just these two examples of persuasion is misleading. Although such emotional mechanisms can replace or outweigh any rational considerations, they need not do so. They can simply serve as reinforcements. To take another example: many bodies in the West have recently been appealing for funds for the relief of famine in poor countries. Their advertisements carry a brief explanation of the point of the appeal, but also, very often, show a picture of a starving child. These pictures are effective. Being striking, they draw attention; being pitiful, they arouse sympathetic feelings; being persuasive, when taken together with the caption and the comment, they help to form a generous attitude towards the aim of the appeal. The advertisement thus exploits the strong effect that a picture of a starving child has upon most people's minds in order to change their attitudes, and so their actions. But to this exploitation of our feelings few of us would take exception; it seems, on the contrary, a perfectly natural and reasonable thing to do. Why then object to the advertisement for the tea or the political party?

The obvious if cynical answer to this question is that we only object to the use of such methods of persuasion when we object or are indifferent to the purpose for which they are being used. We all share the conviction that famine is bad, and think that everything possible should be done to relieve it. Far fewer of us are convinced of the special merits of any political party, fewer still of those of a particular brand of tea. We therefore accept methods of persuasion in the first case that make us suspicious in the other two. And there is some truth in this explanation. We do tend to be uncritical of the means used to persuade other people of the truth of something we implicitly believe: the convinced Conservative is not likely to be worried by the picnic poster. However, there is more in the matter than just prejudice. It is true that pictures of starving children play as directly on our emotions as pictures of romantic scenes; but, still, the picture of a starving child gives a perfectly realistic impression of the situation with which the campaign for famine relief is trying to deal, while the picture of a romantic couple has little or nothing to do with Conservative economic policy. What is objectionable in such cases is not the playing on feelings, nor even the playing on feelings for purposes of which we may happen to disapprove, but doing so by suppressing facts, as in the case of the tea, or by distorting them, as in that of the picnic. When that happens people are led into a certain line of action by misunderstanding, indeed by being deliberately encouraged to misunderstand, its nature and results. Facts disappear into a haze of wishful thinking, attitudes harden into prejudices, and the desire to understand another man's position and reach a measure of agreement with him yields to the resolve to make him fit in with your intentions by any means that come to hand.

Now, if there is one thing clear about the speeches of the ideologists it is that they are meant to influence conduct. The ideologist is no neutral theorist; he wants people to act in certain ways—to make a revolution, to obey the Church —and the object of his speech is to persuade them to do so. Nor are the speeches cool in tone, arguing from the hearer's assumed interests and the facts of the case that he should act in that way out of common sense. Emotion is much in evidence in what they say.

It follows that the very first move in the analysis of an ideology is to separate out for inspection all those of its elements which, like 'free' in the advertisements, exert a direct influence upon our emotions and attitudes through the built-in causal properties of the words employed. This move is not meant to imply that the use of such persuasive forces is always wrong; it is possible, for example, that they are being very properly used in a given case to undermine prejudice against the conclusion of a sound argument. The point is merely that we must get into the way of asking, as a standard precaution, how the persuasive forces of words are being used in each particular case. For if people with different feelings are to co-operate they must learn how to control the influence of feelings, and of words that activate feelings, on their thought. If there are linguistic techniques for creating error we must find techniques for detecting and exposing them, whether they occur in commerce, politics, or ideology.

The Programme of the Communist Party of the Soviet Union, adopted at the 22nd Congress of that party in 1961, contained the fullest and most authoritative statement of its principles made since the death of Stalin. Its theoretical content was, of course, not new. It consisted of the basic ideas of classical Marxism adapted to fit the facts of Eastern Europe, which are very different from those facts of Western Europe that Marx had in mind when he framed his theories. The Communist Party of the Soviet Union had to drag and drive a reluctant peasantry, not lead a revolutionary proletariat; the theory and practice of the party became dictatorial to match its task. Much of that dictatorial quality remained in the new programme, but what was new was the open repudiation of the excesses of Stalinism and the emphasis on the swift approach of a new epoch. In particular, the concluding sentence runs: 'The party solemnly proclaims: the present generation of Soviet people shall live in Communism'—shall live, that is, in that classless society, free from exploitation and oppression, where each will give according to his abilities and receive according to his needs. This transformation of society is therefore scheduled to come towards the end of this century; the programme was concerned with all the preparations for it.

These preparations continue to be arduous, though not so arduous as they have been. Sacrifice and effort are required, as well as widespread understanding of the course to be followed and the gains to be won. The programme therefore does everything it can to carry the reader with it. The Marxist arguments are, of course, deployed at length, and with much repetition. The inevitable breakdown of capitalist society, the inevitable growth of socialist society, the inevitable formation of the scientific and industrial foundations of Communist society: all that is demonstrated once again; and any demonstrations that are made so much of clearly deserve our scrupulous attention. But the programme offers more than arguments. It contains an extraordinary wealth of metaphor. The activities of the party, of the workers and peasants, of the whole Soviet people and of their enemies, are described with a wealth of biological, military, and architectural terms. We are told of 'the decayed capitalist shell', and of the attempts of 'decaying and moribund capitalism' to 'strangle the Soviet state at birth'. We hear of how the 'first contingents of the working class stormed the old world' and 'achieved decisive victories', with the Bolshevik Party as its 'vanguard', and with revolutionary Marxism as both its 'banner' and its 'powerful ideological weapon'. We learn how the October Revolution 'shook the earlier structure of capitalist society to its foundations', how the party took on the task of 'building a socialist society' on 'solid economic foundations', and how 'the magnificent edifice of the new world' is becoming visible in Russia, while the West is limited to 'shoring up the capitalist system'. And all three kinds of metaphor—of life, war, and construction—may come together in a single sentence: 'One third of mankind is building a new life under the banner of scientific socialism.'

What do all these figures of speech contribute to the programme's argument?

To the argument, strictly speaking, they contribute nothing. They do not set out any new facts; nor do they, as metaphors sometimes do, suggest relationships or patterns
amongst facts which cannot yet be grasped directly. Marxists can tell you very well in plainer forms what they think
that they are doing. These metaphors are simply being used
to redescribe that familiar situation in a moving way. The
analogy between an army at war and socialist Russia is
slight; no one could seriously say that the metaphor sheds
much light upon the Russian situation. But if, trading upon
what similarities there are (surrounding enemies, strict discipline), you constantly describe the Soviet situation in military terms you may be able to transfer to it some of the
attitudes those terms embody. Words like 'banner', 'weapon',
'victory' and 'vanguard' are still charged with the aggressive,
spirited feelings that they acquired in earlier days; if we can
be induced to talk regularly of the party as a vanguard and
its programme as a banner we shall transfer to them something of the loyalty that our fighting forbears felt for real
vanguards and real banners. And the same point holds for
the other kinds of metaphor. For example: people feel in
a special way towards things that are dying or decaying. If
people get into the way of describing capitalism as dying or
decaying they automatically transfer those feelings to the
economic institutions of the West.

The use of this kind of rhetorical device is not limited to
works of manifest propaganda, such as a party programme;
it is equally to be found in classical Marxism, in Catholic
writings, and indeed in all ideological productions. Thus
Engels talks of the revolution in terms of the proletariat
'seizing' the means of production. 'Seizing' is a vivid word.
It evokes the assertion of a man's power over his environment in the simplest and most definite way: the grip of the
hand on an object. Engels' use of the word tends therefore
to make people think of the revolution in terms of simple
and immediate mastery; and while the evocation of such
masterful feelings certainly helps the revolutionary to get
his way, the feelings themselves are grotesquely inappropriate to the realities of any revolution. Changing the social

relations of millions of people in millions of ways is very
unlike the grip of a hand on an object. And while the Marxists habitually go to the camp or the workshop for their
pictures, the Catholics go to the family. The Church is described as 'mother and teacher'; the Pope is described as a
'father' who shows 'paternal care' and gives 'fatherly blessing'; the whole universe is represented as a cosmic home in
which men are the children. As analyses of the real situations
that they are used to describe these turns of speech are obviously irrelevant, but no less obviously they help to make
some Catholics feel obedient to the Church, and dependent
on it; and they are doubtless often used with that effect in
mind.

There is therefore a common pattern in these seemingly
so different situations, and it gives rise to a common technique. In each case we have an institution—the party or
the Church—which is dominated by a relatively small number of people—the higher party men, the higher clergy. The
men, being what they are in the institutions, are committed
to inducing very large numbers of their fellow-men to act in
ways to which they are not spontaneously inclined—in-
dustrialising Russia at great personal sacrifice, or conform-
ing, also at some sacrifice, to the Church's conception of the
moral law. Each institution's ideologists maintain that there
are the best possible reasons why people should act in those
ways; whether or not that is the case we shall have to consider. But if there are good reasons the ideologists do not
rely exclusively upon them; they also rely on the emotive
powers of language. The words that we use to describe
situations get charged with the feelings that we normally
experience when we are in those situations. The word 'seize'
is charged with the masterful feeling we experience when we
grasp a smallish object firmly, 'father' with the respect and
trust with which most of us have regarded our male parent.
So strong are these linguistic associations that they pass over
into us with the language we inherit, even if we ourselves
have never had the personal experiences on which they were
originally built up. I have never fought for a banner, but
when anything is called a 'banner' I tend to have a zealous
attitude towards it. That being so, if I am brought to call a
doctrine a banner my zealotry will be encouraged, and if I

am brought to call a member of the clergy 'father' my attitude towards him, whether or not he deserves it, will be
tinted with respect.

So far there have proved to be no differences in technique
between these grand ideological cases of the phenomenon
and the pettier cases drawn from party politics and commerce. Indeed, the technique is identical. The difference only
comes in the use that is made of it. The advertiser, at one
extreme, is only concerned to influence a relatively small
segment of the lives of a relatively minor part of the population. The attitudes he wants to work on play a trivial role
in the life of the individual and his society. Nothing follows
from the fact that I drink one brand of tea rather than another, except the advantage to those who make and sell it.
But the ideologist works at the other end of the scale. He is
concerned with general, pervasive, and powerful attitudes.
A change in my tastes in tea, lets everything else remain
much as it was; a change in my zeal for Marxism or in my
respect for the Church affects every aspect of my life. Only a
small minority will ever be dedicated to a brand of tea, but
ideologies reach such numbers that if they are persuaded, or
even half persuaded, history is changed. But the task of the
ideologist being so much greater than that of the advertising
man, his use of persuasive techniques is necessarily more
systematic. He does not rely on isolated gimmicks to sell his
particular brand of conviction; he has, as we saw in the
Marxist and the Catholic cases, a standard pattern of persuasion—of tendentious metaphors, of emotional associations, of sentimental appeals—in terms of which he handles
all the many matters with which he deals. Selecting certain
particular classes of words—the militant, the filial, or whatever else—he speaks on every topic in these terms. Priests
become fathers, and parties become vanguards. He hopes
thereby to make the attitudes those words embody the standard attitudes with which his hearers face the world, and
the power of such bodies as the Communist Party and the
Catholic Church suggests that in this he is remarkably successful.

And, of course, it is not only those bodies that are organised on the authoritarian lines of the Communist Party or
the Catholic Church that use these techniques with success.
We have seen the British Conservative Party working on the

same lines; more important and more striking are the American Presidents. The common theme of the Presidents is that power, in America, is in the hands of the people; that hostile forces—aristocratic England, slave-owners, monopolists, war-mongers—are working against the people's power; and that the people can assert their natural authority over those forces by voting for the speaker and his party. Now much of this may be perfectly reasonable, in some sense of that term yet to be defined. Slavery was no doubt against the common interests of the American people whom Lincoln was addressing, so that he was perfectly right to urge them to join forces to destroy it. But phrases like 'the will of the people' play, in democratic parlance, the same sort of role that is played, in Marxist parlance, by such a phrase as 'the proletariat seizes power'. We know what it is for an individual to have a will of his own—that is, to be set on his purposes—just as we know what it is to seize something. We also know how nice it is to get one's own way. But what it may be for a people to have a will—a people comprising millions of individuals of all kinds and occupations, scattered over a great area—is a very different question. There is indeed the process of voting, but elections are just about as unlike making up one's mind as seizing political power is unlike seizing a stick. In fact the analogy embodied in the phrase 'the will of the people' is so slight that if the phrase is taken as a serious description of the electoral process it is grossly misleading. But, of course, its primary function in the speeches of politicians is not to provide a realistic description of what goes on in an election. 'The will of the people' carries over with it from the ordinary use of 'will' pleasing suggestions of having power to act and of getting one's own way. To be told that the will of the people is being expressed as one votes is to be given the impression that by voting, more particularly by voting for a certain party, one is getting one's own way: the assertiveness that is within us all is expressed, the frustration that we all often feel in face of the anonymous power of society seems to be overcome, by this trick of identification. Of course, it is not just a trick; my vote exerts an influence, although a small one. But the art of the democratic politician is to overlay the immensely complex process of election, in which the individual voter plays an insignificant role, with a simple picture of personal will, according to which the individual voter plays a decisive role by identification with the politician, his party, and the nation. The sovereign people is as much of a myth as the cosmic family or the vanguard of the proletariat.

The first principle for the analysis of ideologies is consequently to be always on the watch for the persuasive power of language. This power, in itself, is neither good nor bad. It can be used to strengthen and encourage, as well as to confuse and mislead. The important thing is to be alive to it, to detect and understand it, in order to be able to judge it. For one of the most distinctive features of the age in which we live is the immense increase of propaganda. There is more of it now than ever before; it has new media that reach every cranny of our lives; it is conducted on the basis of a scientific analysis of the powers of language and the play of human motives. If therefore we are not to be the puppets of other men we must look to our defences, unmasking the persuasive devices that are used against us, and counteracting them with improved persuasions of our own. We must beat the ideologists at their own game.

But the ideologist's game is subtler yet. While he would not deny off the record that he makes what use he can of the emotivity of words, he would always argue that that fact is of secondary importance. What really matters, he contends, are his substantial arguments; and it is the character of these that we must now consider.

5

The Collapse of Values

COMMON SENSE draws a distinction between our emotions and personal attitudes on the one hand and our values on the other. It also draws a distinction between the kinds of support or argument to which the two are open. The ideologists agree with these distinctions, and then develop them. It is of the essence of ideological thinking to maintain that, over and above any personal feelings, there are such things as values, and that these values can be established by reason. Here, says the ideologist, we abandon the play and counterplay of emotive influences for the solid ground of truth and demonstration. But before studying the ideologist's refinements of these notions we had better look at them as they turn up, quite naturally, in the course of ordinary experience.

The ordinary word 'feeling' means several different, though related, things. If asked for my feelings about capital punishment I may answer that it revolts me, implying that it arouses in me both an unpleasant emotion and a hostile attitude. But I may also answer that I hold the practice wrong, meaning that it goes against my values. Again, many people think that it is right to hang murderers, although they also say, no doubt sincerely, that the idea of an execution is repugnant to them; and Himmler, a man as conscientious as he was misguided, once observed that concentration camps were terrible places and that those who did the loathsome work of running them were heroic. His racial value, monstrous as it was, overrode his tastes. Thus values, whether noble or perverse, seem to be something distinct from emotions and attitudes

The distinction between values and emotions is plain enough. I may be agitated without there being anything that my agitation is about; but values, like attitudes, have objects. I cannot just have an attitude, in myself, as I can have an emotion; it must be set on something, such as pleasure, self-control, or race. Likewise, a value is not merely characteristic of myself; it is something that I hold towards things. The distinction between attitudes and values is therefore much less obvious than that between both and the emotions. However, it is held to be just as real. I may be keen on swimming or fed-up with television without in any way making a principle of my positive or negative feelings, and so without implicitly demanding that other people should feel as I do. Indeed, without changing my own attitudes I may expressly allow, and often do, that they are by no means incumbent on anyone else. They are simply my own preferences, and that is that. If, however, I go further and say that one ought to swim, because it is good for health, or that one ought to keep abreast of television, because of its political importance, I am not merely saying that I have favourable attitudes towards those things. Indeed, as in those examples of capital punishment and the concentration camps, my personal feelings towards them may be unfavourable; I could well say that one ought to go in for them even though I may have come to dislike them. Moreover, when I say 'I ought' I am no longer simply speaking for myself, as I am when I say 'I like', but, implicitly, for people in general; and the same is true when I use such words as 'good' or 'right' or any of their opposites. In all such cases I am putting forward a rule that we should observe, or an aim that we should strive for, rather than merely indicating what I myself prefer. These words, in fact, have as their commonest function the expression of principles or ideals—things, that is, that we insist upon. What is asserted by these means are values for people, not just feelings of our own, and these values are alleged to hold no matter whether anyone, including ourselves, either likes them or does not.

This, then, is the commonsense distinction between personal attitudes and values, and whatever must ultimately be made of it there is plainly some distinction here. 'Wrong', for instance, carries a significance that 'disagreeable' or 'inconvenient' do not. There is therefore no harm in using the term 'value' to designate that additional significance, so long as nothing is assumed about what exactly it may be—nothing, in particular, about the alleged rationality of values. That granted, we can use the concept of value to analyse further the word 'free', so crucial to the ideologists.

For while 'free' certainly has an emotive force and serves to convey our personal attitudes, it plainly also serves to convey our values. Indeed, some of our deepest and strongest values are usually conveyed by this particular word. When an Englishman says sincerely of his island that it is a free country his heart will no doubt beat faster and his personal affection for his home be expressed; but, in addition, he will have given the world to understand that he puts a high value on the constitutional arrangements of English society. He will have implied that constitutional arrangements are, in general, things of great importance, and have further declared that those particular arrangements are good, though they may not be perfect. Of course, he may have made the remark casually or insincerely, so that one would in fact be mistaken in concluding from what he had said that he would sacrifice his interests for the safety of the realm; but, levity and hypocrisy apart, the natural conclusion from his remark is that he would do so, if necessary, and that he thinks that other people have a duty to do likewise. Sometimes, at least, 'freedom' is thus a value word; it serves to express more than our emotions and our tastes; it serves to express our beliefs, often our deep convictions, as to what should and what should not be done.

To say, however, that 'freedom' is a value word, serving to express our beliefs as to what men should strive for and avoid, is not to say very much about it. How, for example, does 'free' compare with 'good', the commonest value word of all? It is plain that 'free' is much less comprehensive. I can speak up for anything by means of 'good'. There are good pictures, good motives, good intellects, good friends, good arguments; but 'free motives' or 'free friends' are phrases without meaning. On the other hand, 'good', with some additional phrase, can usually do the work of 'free'. A free country—as the true-born Englishman intends the phrase—is a country with good arrangements and institutions with respect to public assembly, the expression of opinion, the rule of law and civil rights generally. 'Good' is, in fact, as the dictionary puts it, the most general adjective of commendation; 'free' by contrast is restricted. There must be some particular class of situations with respect to which alone it can properly be used to express our sense of values.

But 'free' is by no means as restricted in its range of uses as are the great majority of value words. 'Brave', for example, is a value word. If I call a man brave I am not merely expressing a favourable attitude of my own towards him, as I would be if I said that I was his supporter or friend; I am saying that his character, in a certain respect, is what all our characters should be. The respect in question is that of endurance in the face of pain or danger. That 'brave' attaches value to such conduct, and not merely favour, becomes plain with the reflection that if such endurance increases beyond a certain point we cease to speak of it as 'bravery' and use perhaps 'self-torture' or 'foolhardiness' instead, words that manifestly convey condemnation rather than mere dislike. And that 'brave' can only be significantly used to commend cases of endurance (of a certain degree) is shown by the fact that nonsense results when we use it to commend anything else. What could be meant by a brave motive or argument, unless that what was really being called brave was, say, the actions of avowing the motive or of advancing the argument? And there are many words like 'brave': 'generous', 'malicious', 'considerate', 'casual' . . . the list could run into hundreds. How does 'free' compare with these?

Plainly, if the range of 'free' is narrower than that of 'good' it is wider than that of 'brave'. As well as speaking of a free country, I can speak of woman's freedom in modern society, of academic, religious, or cultural freedom, of freedom from fear or want or war, and so on around the whole horizon of human actions. In each case I am speaking up for something as being good for man; a value is at stake, not my own personal preferences merely. But what am I speaking up for? It seems clear that there is nothing common to all these situations that is anything like so definite and concrete as there is in the case of 'brave'; but still there must be something common to them all, some restriction on the range of things that I can properly commend as free, some feature whose necessary presence marks off 'free' from 'good'.

It seems that in all these cases we are dealing with some kind of human activity, and some kind of restriction to which it may or may not be subject. Human beings are capable, according to circumstances, of extraordinarily diverse behaviour. This behaviour we classify. Thus we distinguish sexual from aesthetic or political behaviour; inside sexual behaviour we distinguish the heterosexual from the homosexual and the rest; inside each of these we introduce still further distinctions. Such classes of behaviour can be restricted or promoted in many different ways. We can physically prevent people from doing things, enact laws to punish those who do, and bring children up to feel guilty when they contemplate them; conversely, we can encourage or compel. Bearing in mind that 'free' is a value word, let us then suppose ourselves convinced that it is good that people should be able to exercise a certain capacity, for example, to worship God or worship no God, as they please. That being so, we shall deplore anything—a law, for example, or the pressure of public opinion—that makes it difficult or impossible for people to worship or not worship as they see fit. If then we suppose such a restriction to be absent or removed we shall say that the society in question enjoys religious freedom, meaning by that phrase that the members of that society are able to exercise the capacity, which we think good, to worship or not at pleasure. To generalise the point: it seems that the normal use of the word 'free', when functioning as a value word, is to serve to express our belief that it is good that some human capacity or other should not be restricted in certain ways. Thus by women's freedom is meant that they are not subjected economically, politically, and legally to men; by academic freedom that teachers do not get instructions from the state as to what should and what should not be taught, especially in matters of religion and politics; by freedom from want, that men are not inhibited by poverty; it being understood in all these cases that the activities in question are held to be good or right, and therefore the restriction of them bad or wrong.

As for this distinction between good and right, or between bad and wrong, as different forms of value, the case appears to be this. What we think valuable may be either the doing of a certain thing in certain circumstances or some more comprehensive state of affairs in which no immediate reference to actions is involved. Values of the first kind we call principles, of the second kind, ideals; we use 'right' to characterise actions which agree with our principles and 'good' to characterise situations that agree with our ideals.

Examples of principles are telling the truth and keeping promises; examples of ideals are the disposition of forgivingness and the state of peace. A principle, that is, commends a single type of action, while an ideal commends a state of affairs to which many types of action make their contribution. The principle of truthfulness involves telling the truth; the ideal of forgivingness involves, perhaps, saying 'I forgive' on appropriate occasions, but it also involves doing a selection of many other things, such as being gentle, or behaving as if nothing had been done. In these terms 'free', on the whole, serves to express ideals. The freedom of women or of teachers refers to whole states of affairs covering a wide diversity of actions, rather than to a single type of action, like telling the truth. But this point is not of great importance here. What matters is that 'free' is a value word, not what kind of value word it is.

Our theoretical results so far are therefore these. 'Free' and the like are emotive words in that they convey a sense of excitement and release. They are also words that are normally used to express our attitudes of being personally for or against, of liking or disliking, certain types of thing, person, or situation. Finally, they are words that serve to express our beliefs that certain types of situation are good or bad, irrespective of who is concerned or what their tastes may be. What, then, is common to these types of situation? When we use 'free' rather than 'good' to express our valuations what we normally have in mind is some human capacity to act and some factor that can restrict its exercise. And though this latter point arose in connection with values rather than with attitudes, it plainly holds for them as well. We use 'free' to express how we personally feel about something only when it is the exercise of some capacity that is in question; otherwise we use 'pleasant' or 'nice' (or 'good', in that one of its several senses in which, no longer expressing a general value, it is roughly equivalent to the other two). And the use of 'free' to express our attitudes and values goes far to explain, as can now be seen more clearly, how it comes by its emotive force. On the one hand it is agreeable to think of people, ourselves particularly, acting as they please; on the other it is stirring to think of them making sacrifices for their convictions as to the right of some human capacity to unrestricted exercise. And so, by being used to handle situations that awaken these emotions in us, 'free' itself gets connected with the emotions and tends thenceforward to arouse them even when the situation to which it is applied would not do so by itself. You can sell anything with 'free'.

So whatever the point of the distinction between personal attitudes and values proves to be, the force of the ideologist's key term 'free' certainly depends upon it. When the ideologist tells me that freedom is this or freedom is that he seems to be doing more than express his feelings and influence mine. But what more is he doing? He says himself that he is stating some ideal or rational principle of conduct. The American Declaration of Independence sets out what it calls 'self-evident' truths', and the other ideologists make a like claim to rationality. And this is plainly the key point. If the claim to rationality fails, then values lose their apparent objectivity and are reduced to statements of mere preference; ideologies, at the same time, lose their look of truth and demonstation and become no more than the manifestation of feelings that we know they are in part. What, then, is the case with the rationality of values?

If I tell you that I like something, or have any other favourable attitude towards it, such as interest or affection, and you ask me why, the only answers that I can give are, first, what it is about the thing that makes me like it and, second, how it is that I have come to do so. I can tell you that what I like about sunny weather is more the colour than the heat; I can also perhaps explain how colour has come to play a large part in my life. This second kind of answer admittedly is often hard to give. While we can tell how we come by acquired tastes, generally speaking we cannot do much more about our likes and dislikes than simply confirm that that is what they are. Indeed, we are often at a loss to provide even the first answer, finding it hard to say what it is about a thing that makes us like it. Why, after all, do I prefer coffee to tea for breakfast? Why am I attracted to Miss A rather than to Miss B? But still the two kinds of answer are available in principle, however elusive they may be in practice; and physiologists and psychologists can often carry on the analysis where we leave off, showing what really attracts us and why it does so. There may be a chemical basis for my preference for a kind of drink, while my attraction to a particular girl may be due to an elaborate process of social conditioning during my early years, of which any account that I can give of her amiable qualities will, to the analytic eye, be so much rationalisation. But be that as it may, all that can ever be done to explain my tastes is for it to be stated more accurately what they are, and for hypotheses to be advanced and tested as to how they come to be so. That done, there is nothing more to be said. I cannot, for instance, be asked to justify my tastes, though I can sometimes be asked to justify my allowing them to develop or my yielding to them now that they have done so. My tastes are my tastes, and that is that.

If, however, I go beyond saying that I like a thing and pronounce it to be good, in the sense of valuable, I seem to lay myself open to further questions. The first two questions can still be asked, and often must be. What is it about the thing, what are the properties that it possesses, that make you call it good? How did you come by the conviction that it is? But when these questions have been dealt with the matter does not end. Why, I may be asked, do you call it good? However you have come by the conviction, what entitles you to say that a thing that possesses just those properties is valuable? We can state and explain our values equally with our tastes, but we can also be required to say what justifies them.

This liability is not surprising. We distinguish values from tastes precisely by the fact that they are put forward as holding for people, rather than as merely being characteristic of ourselves. The whole point of advancing from saying that a thing is nice to saying that it is good is precisely to make a claim upon the actions of ourselves and others, no matter what our or their tastes may be. We are being asked, if necessary, to overrule our inclinations. So what could be more natural than that we should be required to explain not just the content and origin of such a claim, but the ground on which it rests? When a man lays down principles or sets up ideals argument must be allowed to follow; for if the layer-down or setter-up declines to enter into argument what he is really doing is to admit that his so-called principles and ideals are no more than his personal tastes, dressed up in solemn and misleading form.

It is, then, of the very essence of values—as they are commonly conceived—that support for them may always be demanded and that an attempt to provide it must be made. In practice, and for many reasons, the attempt may fail; but it cannot be declined in theory. To do so is to reduce the value to a taste.

For the sake of argument let us now suppose this point conceded. Values, as such, require support. But how are they to be supported?

Consider an example. Suppose that we believe in the emancipation of women and express our opinion by saying that women are free in England as they were not a hundred years ago and are not now in Switzerland, where they do not have the vote, or in India, where their marriages are often still arranged. Since 'free' is operating as a value word, to say that women are free is to say that the situation of women is as it should be with regard, by implication, to their political, economic, and personal rights. This is a claim on conduct. By it stand condemned an electorate that denies the vote to women or a class of parents who oblige their daughters to accept husbands. But why should these people yield to my claim any more than I to theirs? Some support, some argument, is obviously required. What form must it take? It seems that further facts should be produced; the consequences to women of the two regimes need to be established. Take the case of arranged marriage. Amongst the consequences of obligatory marriage will be that some women have to marry who would rather stay single and that others who want to marry yet have to marry men whom they dislike; on the other hand it may be held that obligatory marriage is an integral part of the organisation of a certain form of family, which would disintegrate without it. It may also be held that it relieves girls of a difficult responsibility. Suppose, for the sake of argument, that these facts are conceded. Thus one who believes in obligatory marriage, while pointing out that the girls have more say in the matter than might be supposed by an observer from outside, will concede that a girl may often be obliged to give up a man she loves to marry another whom she does not, even one by whom she is actively repelled. But, this concession made, suppose it is simply said, so what? What is the relevance? What do the girl's tastes matter?—the argument, clearly, has to be resumed. One possible direction would be to point to further facts. It might be argued that sexual tastes are both strong and lasting, so that much unhappiness will be caused by forcing anything upon them; but this again might be conceded by the believer in arranged marriage, who could still say, so what? What does that matter? Plainly, each party is making assumptions of some further kind that give the admitted facts a different bearing on the case. Thus the emancipator of women is assuming that no one ought to be obliged to have sexual relations with any one he or she dislikes, that avoidable unhappiness should not be incurred, and that the family structure of which obligatory marriage forms a part is either of no comparable value or positively bad. But all these are assumptions of value, not of fact; and the suggestion is therefore forced upon us that when we have to support a value we must bring forward not only further facts but further values; not only further facts about the thing whose value is at stake, but further ideals and principles that make those facts relevant to valuation. This suggestion, if borne out, would plainly be of great importance.

It is certainly not the case that assertions of every kind must number ideals and moral principles amongst the assumptions that support them. If the question is whether water is essential for life, all I have to do is to show by experiment that while the amount of moisture required by living things varies widely, nothing can in fact survive without any moisture at all, and then, if possible, to reinforce the observed facts by an explanation of the part played by water in the processes of life. But the force of such an explanation stems ultimately from further observations, suitably generalised into a theory and then re-tested; we can therefore say that the only support that the original assertion needs and can receive is the support of observation. Of course, the facts that are actually observable at any time may not suffice to establish or refute the original assertion, nor even to increase or diminish its probability. A suitable technique of observation may not yet have been evolved: before the lunik it was impossible to prove, although it was reasonable to believe, that there were mountains on the other side of the moon. But if a statement is to qualify as a statement of fact at all it must at least be possible to suggest the sort of observations that would, in principle, confirm or disconfirm it; and if favourable observations are forthcoming the statement is to that extent supported, quite irrespective of any convictions we may have about right and wrong or good and bad. And experience in fact shows that people with utterly different values can come to agree, by experiment and observation, on a limitless range of factual matters, from the structure of the atom to the structure of the heavens. That is the possibility of which natural science is the realisation.

The analysis of the role played by value assumptions in arguments intended to support a value conclusion must therefore take place against the background of a kind of argument, factual argument, in which value assumptions seem to play no part at all. Is it, then, really the case that where we are arguing to support a value—say, the freedom of women—we must assume at least one other—say that people should not be made to have sexual relations with those whom they dislike?

It sometimes appears as if such assumptions are not necessary. Thus we might argue: arranged marriages are liable to be offensive to the pair so married; whatever is liable to be offensive is bad; arranged marriages are therefore bad. The statement that arranged marriages are offensive may then be held to record the observed matter of fact that they do actually cause offence, and since the statement that whatever is offensive is bad does no more than spell out part of the accepted meaning of 'offensive', it may be urged that the badness of arranged marriages follows just as much from observed facts as does the necessity of water for life. But this opinion is mistaken. The conclusion of the argument certainly follows from its premises, and the second premise —that what is offensive is by definition bad—is certainly correct; but the first premise, that arranged marriages are liable to be offensive, is by no means just a statement of fact. All that is undoubtedly a fact here is that some arranged marriages are disliked by those for whom they are arranged. The argument is then destroyed by a dilemma. If we restate the first premises as 'arranged marriages are sometimes disliked', then the conclusion no longer follows, since many things that are disliked are right or good: did not the Nazis dislike the destruction of their state and party? But if we strengthen the first premise so as to make the conclusion follow and say that arranged marriages tend to be justifiably disliked (which is roughly what 'offensive' means) then the argument assumes precisely what it sets out to prove, namely that the dislike in question is justifiable. In fact, the appearance that that argument has of proceeding from a fact and a definition to a value is delusive. We do not at first notice that 'offensive' is itself a value word, just as we may not notice the same thing in the case of 'brave' or 'kind'; and so we do not notice that the crucial step of valuation has already been taken when the practice has been called offensive. The 'argument' therefore establishes nothing; it only spells out what has already been assumed.

It follows that those who contend that values can be proved from facts alone must be compelled to scrutinise their premises and make quite sure that they contain no words, such as 'offensive', which, like 'unpleasant', have the appearance of being factual but are often more. This is harder than it sounds. It is remarkable how many words have implications of value in addition to their implications of fact. 'Rude', 'considerate', 'heartless', 'reliable', 'mean', 'sociable', 'enterprising', 'cultured', 'ignorant', 'black', 'white', 'colonial', 'empire', 'aristocrat', 'worker', 'thrift'; hundreds of words, in fact, by which we describe men's characters and situations carry an implication that the things referred to are good or bad, right or wrong, superior or inferior. This is a convenient arrangement of language; it enables us both to describe and to appraise something by a single word. And the fact that a language affords this simple means of attaching a particular degree of appraisal to a particular kind of thing reflects the fact that the society to which the language belongs has that particular value, and so needs a word to express it economically. Naturally, therefore, such words go out of use as society changes. 'Piety', 'gravity', 'thrift', 'noble', 'gallant': such words are as obsolete morally as the puritanical and aristocratic societies to which they belonged; 'reliable', 'rational', 'enterprising' are still with us, the values they embody being typical of our society. The mere learning of some such words and the exclusion of others is in fact one of the most powerful means of education in the ideals and principles of a society.

That being so it will certainly often be difficult to make

sure that no words implicitly containing values feature in
the premises from which a value is alleged to follow, and so
to test the view that values, like theories, can be supported
simply by appeal to fact. With care, however, and some
long-windedness, this can be done; and when it has been the
resulting argument invariably proves to be defective. 'Homosexuality is unnatural, and therefore wrong'? Replace 'unnatural' by 'not the sexual practice by which the human
race is perpetuated' and the conclusion obviously does not
follow. 'Unnatural' carries with it an implication of wrong-
ness, so that to call homosexuality unnatural begs the question; when that implication has been dropped, as in the extended phrase, the argument breaks in two. 'Uncivilised
peoples are not fit to rule themselves'? Replace 'uncivilised'
by 'not following the European (or the Chinese) way of life'
and the argument collapses, for why should not other civilisations be politically autonomous? Replace it by 'politically
immature' and the argument becomes the trivial 'politically
immature peoples are not fit to rule themselves'. 'Uncivilised'
carries with it just that implication of political inferiority
that makes the argument circular. And so the examples could
go on for ever. To cut them short: those who believe that
values can be proved by facts alone are hereby challenged
to produce a single case in which the facts are truly facts
and not values in disguise, the conclusion a value, and the
inference compelling. Until they have done so it must be
assumed that in order to support a value we need facts indeed, but also something else: a value or a set of values that
connects these facts with the values that are to be supported,
as the principle 'people ought not to be made to have sexual
experience against their will' connects the alleged facts of
arranged marriage with the value of emancipation. And
when we bear in mind the great number of facts that are
potentially relevant to any given value, and must therefore
be appraised themselves if they are to become really relevant, it looks as if what must be assumed in an argument
for any value is a world of other values.

This result, compelling in itself, raises at once the most
fundamental of all the difficulties attending arguments about
value in general and therefore about freedom in particular.
If we hold that values, as opposed to tastes, must be supported, and also that an essential part of that support are

further values, does it not follow that all arguments about what is good or bad or right or wrong are circular? Challenged to support my principle that arranged marriage is bad, I produce evidence to show that arranged marriage tends to involve unwilling sexual intercourse; I maintain the further value that unwilling intercourse is bad; and I conclude that arranged marriage is to be condemned. But the supporting value can be questioned just as much as can the value that was to be supported. What justifies my condemnation of unwilling intercourse? At this point I may appeal directly to a more general principle, asserting that all interference with the body of an unwilling and innocent person is wrong. If the person in question is guilty of a crime, force may be used against him, but then only in minimal and regulated ways. This general principle obviously covers many more things than unwilling intercourse of the kind that sometimes attends an arranged marriage. It covers, for instance, rape, unlawful arrest, assault, and robbery with violence. As these examples suggest, it is a principle that many people hold to be of fundamental importance; so much so, indeed, that they might hardly understand what you were getting at if you questioned its validity. But such a question can be raised. Let anyone who doubts that read Homer or Elizabethan tragedy; he will find that men of high intelligence have judged violence in a way very different from that now current in the Western world, condoning and even praising acts that seem to us detestable. But if we cannot regard our principle of greatly reduced and closely regulated violence as axiomatic we must argue in support of it; and we can only do so first by pointing to the consequences of allowing force a looser rein—consequences both to the character of the agent and to the lives of those his violence strikes—and then by bringing further values to bear upon them. But by now it is plain that this procedure is interminable. We can only support one value by relying on at least one other; but that other can always be questioned in its turn. And from this the sceptical conclusion seems to follow that since no single value is secure, the whole structure of our principles and our ideals is built on sand.

This conclusion, if sound, would be disastrous for the ideologist. Amongst the many things that he would have us accept is a certain image of himself. This image has nothing to do with advertising or propaganda; we are not to see the ideologist as a man who is just getting at us with techniques of persuasion. Rather, we are to see him as a man of science: a man who is certainly telling us how we should act, but who is only doing so on rational grounds, acceptable to all. To that image the concept of a value is the key. For a value, precisely, is a statement which purports both to prescribe how we should act and to be based on grounds that we can all accept, as rational beings. It follows that if this claim to rationality is shaken, the concept of value is shaken too; and that if the concept of value falls, the dignity of the ideologist falls with it. He can no longer speak with the authority of science but only with the wiles of the ad-man. Naturally, therefore, the ideologists have been at great pains to establish that claim to rationality on which the concept of value and their own authority depend. In particular, each of our three main ideologists has developed a theory on this point. According to the American Declaration of Independence, the fundamental values are self-evident: a faculty of intuition is called in to explain our knowledge of values. The Catholic makes values depend on God: moral and social principles are the laws laid down by God for man. The Marxist makes values depend on history: a value sets out what a particular class in history has to strive for in order to carry out its necessary role. We must now observe how, one after another, these theories fail.

'We hold these truths to be self-evident,' said the founding fathers of the American Constitution, and went on to enumerate the values on which that constitution was supposed to rest. That, in embryo, is what has been called the intuitionist theory of values. The intuitionist maintains that we can just see what is good and what is bad, much as we can just see what is black and what is white. He concedes that values cannot be seen in exactly the same way as sounds or colours; they cannot be observed by the five senses as can the properties with which science deals. But why, he argues, should the five senses be the only channels of immediate knowledge? After all, we know that $2+2=4$, quite independently of anything we can perceive by sense. No conceivable observation could ever shake our assurance of that truth; therefore, it cannot rest on observation. It is, on the contrary, a self-evident truth, and its existence is enough to prove that we must have another source of immediate knowledge than our physical organs. We must have a power of intellectual, as well as of sensuous, intuition. But if we must assume a power of intellectual intuition in order to account for the existence of mathematical knowledge, why should we not use it, as we can, to solve the problem of moral knowledge? For here too we have knowledge that cannot be shaken by any observation, and cannot therefore rest on observation. If the fact that putting two pairs of drops of water in a spoon and getting one rather than four does not shake my faith in the truth of $2 + 2 = 4$, why should the fact that some people get pleasure by causing pain shake my faith that cruelty is wrong? Of course, it does nothing of the kind; and the reason in the moral case is the same as in the mathematical: we know these truths, independently of all experience, by our intellectual perception of the inherent connectedness of things.

It is easy to show that the intuitionist theory of mathematical knowledge is mistaken, but to do so would not be relevant here, for however much is made of the comparison, the intuitionist view of values can be maintained even if the analogous view of mathematics has to be abandoned. Moral intuitionism must therefore be considered on its own. Superficially it is attractive. If we take for example the practice of mass killing, which most of us now feel has nothing to commend it, whether in its old religious or in its modern racial forms, we are inclined to say that one can just see that it is wrong and that everyone who thinks otherwise is morally blind. Auschwitz was simply and visibly wrong, no more, no less. And this way of speaking about the basis of our values seems to do full justice to our conviction that they are more than personal tastes; for it represents them as truths which stand impartially above us all, and give us common rules to live by. But these appearances are delusive. In the first place, while the theory seems convincing when we restrict our view to situations that are morally simple (either in that one value only is relevant to them, or in that all the relevant values point the same way, or in that any value that contradicts the rest is felt to be of small importance), it ceases to be so immediately we consider those situations, just—alas!—as common, in which values of roughly equal importance point in opposite directions. When I have to choose between telling a lie and hurting feelings, or between the freedom of women to choose their husbands and the freedom of parents to control their children, it is no help to be told that moral principles are self-evident truths. We all know that in such cases what is self-evident to one person may be ridiculous to another; and, anyway, if we continue to speak in terms of self-evidence at all the need is for some way of deciding between one claim to self-evidence and the next. Faced by the conflict of moral principles and ideals, as embodied in different individuals, groups, societies, or civilisations, the intuitionist can only go on saying that one party—his own, of course—is right, and that the others are morally defective. If, once the facts of the case have been clarified, they do not see the moral truth that he does, there must be something wrong with their powers of moral intuition: they must be value-blind, as some people are colour-blind. But this comparison proves fatal to the intuitionist case. It breaks down at the crucial point. There are objective tests of colour-blindness which the sufferer can and must accept as decisive. It can be proved to him that other people can make discriminations between colours that he cannot. Other people, between whom collusion has been made impossible, will pick out the same patterns on suitably coloured cards, while he is quite unable to detect them. 'Colour-blind' has therefore an objective meaning; in saying that someone is defective in this respect we do not rely merely on the strength of our own conviction of the differences of colours; we can prove that these differences are real by using them to make regular distinctions between objects. But the moral intuitionist can offer no further proof that those who disagree with him are morally blind than the mere fact that they disagree with him; and they have just as much right to say the same of him as he of them. That is not to say that the phrase 'moral blindness' is without meaning. It can reasonably be used to describe the situations, for example, of the demented or the senile, people who can make no moral distinctions at all because of some general defectiveness of mind. What is fallacious is to use it of people who can make moral distinctions but who make them differently from oneself. To do that is simply to assert that one is right, without giving any reason for one's assertion. In fact, the intuitionist theory of values is only distinguished by its highfaluting language from the theory that values are matters of personal taste. While making much of the objectivity of values it collapses, under pressure, into an extreme subjectivism.

Faced by the same problem of finding a basis for human values independent of men's various tastes and preferences, the Catholic takes a different course. On his view God created man and—naturally—prescribed how he should live. Values are God's commands. They are therefore unchanging and universal: unchanging because God himself is immutable; universal because God did not create some men, or groups of men, but man. Therefore man's moral business is first to discover God's commands and then to obey them. But the difficulty, precisely, is to discover what God has commanded. Different individuals and societies offer us flatly contradictory versions; and while in the case of a mortal ruler it is always possible in principle to find out what he has laid down—one can ask him, or ask his ministers, or watch them act—God's commands are systematically elusive. Just because God is God, a supernatural being, his decisions are not to be discovered by natural means. It is true that Catholic theologians have denied this, asserting for example that the principle of monogamy can be read out of the facts as the only proper principle for organising human reproduction; but if, following the lines of the earlier discussion, we take care that no question-begging terms are allowed to creep into our description of the biological facts, it will be found that there is nothing in them that logically implies the superiority or necessity of monogamy, let alone what the Catholic also claims, the immorality in all circumstances of divorce and contraception. If we are then told that failing reason we must use the supernatural means of faith instead, then, in face of the great diversity of faiths, each with its own moral deliverances, we are bound to ask how we are to know which faith is the true one. And if we are told that a particular man, tradition or institution, a church for instance, is the repository of faith, we must again ask how to decide between any one such claim and others like it. These questions, plainly, are unanswerable; the essence of a faith is to be accountable to nothing outside itself; all that the theologian can do is to evade such demands as impressively as possible by appealing to the peculiar mysteries of his own conviction. But the effect of this manœuvre is, as in the case of intuitionism, to reduce judgments of value to expressions of taste. The search for objectivity ends in caprice; and caprice is not less objectionable—if anything it is more—when dressed up in solemn form.

But not only do intuitionist and theological theories of value have a common failure; their failures have a common cause. On closer inspection they appear to share the thesis that some values at least are absolute, in the sense of being universally and necessarily true. Given, however, by the previous argument, that they cannot be shown to be absolutely true by being shown to follow necessarily from facts—for no value follows necessarily from facts alone—then they must either be self-evident or be shown to follow from statements of some other kind, perhaps from statements about God. Experience shows, however, that there is just as much disagreement about what is self-evident and what is theologically true as there is about what is good and bad, so that the attempt to base morality either upon intuition or upon religious faith leaves the value problem exactly where it was. And it was in a most unsatisfactory state. For if we assume, with these two theories, that for a value to be distinguished from a taste it must be absolute, then in any but the simplest situations, in which there is really no moral problem at all, what we have is two supposedly absolute values in collision. Whatever interpretation we finally put on it, the very essence of the moral life lies in deciding which ideal or principle must be given up when the facts make it impossible for them all to be satisfied. Is it better, if you live in a poor society with a high birth-rate, to encourage contraception or acquiesce in starvation? The fundamental weakness of the absolutist position is that it prevents us from thinking out a problem like that. When, as constantly happens, the facts of the world bring our principles into contradiction, then the absolutist either must pretend that the problem does not exist, which is caprice in disguise, or else must qualify at least one of his principles in such a way as to restore their consistency; he must accept contraception when the alternative is mass starvation, or maintain that starvation is the lesser of two evils.

But absolute principles, in the nature of the case, cannot be qualified. What therefore happens under the pressure of circumstances is that the absolute values are maintained in principle while expediency rules in practice. Contraception continues to be excluded in principle, but a meaningless distinction is drawn between 'natural' methods, which are permissible, and 'artificial' methods, which are not. Man is said to have a natural right to political equality, but effective means are found to deny to American Negroes in reality what in theory they enjoy. But with this the claim that values are rational has broken down completely. All that is left is myth, evasion, and hypocrisy: the myths—in moral form—of certain powerful groups and institutions; the evasion of all awkward discrepancies between the myths and fact; the hypocrisy of those who use the name of reason to advance their special interests.

At this point the American ideologist, if he had the chance, would retort that he was being unfairly treated. It is true, he would say, that some of his colleagues have believed that fundamental values are self-evident truths, known by intuition; but liberal democracy does not stand or fall with this philosophical position. For liberal democrats—American or other—have as often, perhaps more often, justified their social principles by appeal to the quality of life that is achieved by living in accordance with them. This view, when systematised in England in the early nineteenth century, was called 'utilitarianism'. It has remained the standard position of English radicalism, whether liberal or socialist, since that time. But is it any better at explaining the alleged rationality of values than the absolutist theories that have been dismissed? According to utilitarianism the crucial point to consider in adopting and applying principles is the effect that the resulting behaviour would have upon the happiness and suffering of those affected by it. In proportion as actions tend to cause happiness and diminish suffering the principles that counsel them should be adopted; in proportion as they do not the principles should be rejected. How else, utilitarians argue, can any reasonable person think? Is any man prepared to say that a principle should be adopted quite irrespective of its effects upon happiness? Surely not! Anyone, at least, who maintained such a barbarous position would be putting himself beyond the pale of rational discussion. But if once the general happiness is admitted to be relevant to our choice of principles, it must be admitted to be the only thing that is relevant at all; for supposing it conflicted with some other consideration, then anyone who gave precedence to that other consideration would be guilty of the same barbarity. No one, in fact, who considers the point coolly and rationally can possibly put any consideration above the productiveness of happiness as a ground for adopting a principle or applying it in a particular way. This supreme principle can be applied in all circumstances; so applied, it can solve the problem of conflicting principles that absolutist theories left unsolved behind them. Circumstances, let us suppose, have thrown two of our principles into conflict; if we are not to evade the issue at least one of them must be withdrawn or qualified. But this necessity, fatal to the absolutist, is normal to the utilitarian. For him no principle in itself is sacred; the authority of principles is due solely to the supposed utility of acting on them. So if two principles conflict we have only to investigate the effects upon human happiness of acting in one way or the other, or in some third way obtained by qualification of them both. It need not be assumed that this investigation will be easy, or that it will always reach a clear result. It is often very hard to discover the effects of a practice and of its alternatives upon the happiness of those involved; and even if one thinks one has succeeded one may find that the actions are evenly balanced in this respect. But that is merely to say that thinking about values is always difficult and often inconclusive, which no one in his senses would deny; it by no means excludes the equally undeniable fact that very often the effects of a practice upon happiness are clear and decisive.

Actions and principles are therefore right and wrong in so far as they tend to increase happiness and diminish suffering. What, says the utilitarian, could be plainer or more rational than that? If anyone has an alternative let him produce it; but until this challenge has been met we can safely go ahead on the assumption that we now know how to frame a scheme of conduct. And framing schemes of conduct is still perfectly in order; even though we have a supreme principle, we still heed particular principles. If it is the case that in almost all societies, or anyway in the circumstances of our own society, a certain pattern of action does tend on the whole to produce happiness or diminish suffering, then by and large we can safely act on the principle that prescribes that pattern of action, without on each occasion trying to work out the consequences. The advantage of particular principles is precisely that they enable us to conserve our intellectual energy for difficult occasions; and this advantage is especially great in the case of those principles, like that of telling the truth, which all experience shows to be generally conducive to human happiness, and on which we can therefore generally rely. And so, while the rational man reviews his principles from time to time in the light of utility, he does not always try to think directly in its terms, dispensing with principles altogether, but rather reserves the appeal to utility for times of doubt and crisis, when his standard principles, left to themselves, would land him in confusion and reduce him to caprice.

That this theory about the rationality of values makes an advance on absolutist theories is evident from a simple logical consideration. A principle ('when questioned, always tell the truth'; 'once married, never contemplate divorce') gives a prescription as to what should or should not be done in specified circumstances. But the action so prescribed (telling the truth, refusing divorce) cannot in fact be separated from its consequences in a particular case; in committing oneself to the action one is committing oneself to its results, whatever they may be, in so far as they can reasonably be foreseen. Whoever wills the means wills the likely end. If, being a member of a conspiracy, I am arrested by the secret police, am questioned by them, and, by telling the truth, incriminate my friends, I shall be killing them as surely as if my own finger was on the trigger. The principle of saving life is just as relevant here as that of truthfulness. There is absolutely no reason—prejudice apart—why one should consider the action exclusively in the light of just one of the principles that apply to it; to do so, indeed, is precisely to turn a principle into a prejudice, a general guide to action into an unthinking habit. In taking a difficult decision it is therefore necessary to balance one principle with another in the light of an ulterior end. The great service that utilitarianism renders is to remind us that a principle is not a railway track, not even a roadway; at best it is a provisional line of march.

But when we advance into the positive contentions of the theory, difficulties arise. We are told that in choosing how to follow and combine our lines of march we must always and only consider the effects of our choice on human happiness. At first sight that looks clear enough. We usually know when people are happy and when they are not. We usually know when one person is happier than another. We are often prepared to put a degree on this and to say that he is very much happier, or only just a little. And we are also prepared, though with more caution, to do the same for groups of people : the finance minister who proposes to take money from the rich and to give it to the poor in the shape of welfare services probably makes a judgment of that kind. But is he right to do so? Can one seriously claim that one can add up the satisfactions and dissatisfactions of large numbers of people and determine what the balance is? The claim certainly does sound unplausible when put in that way; but perhaps nothing more is being said against utilitarianism here than that the issues of life are so often obscure that no one decision can be rationally preferred to any other. an observation that is hardly news and is certainly no objection to utilitarianism. For if the balance of happiness and unhappiness is sometimes uncertain it is also sometimes perfectly clear. Is it not, for example, perfectly clear that the inhabitants of concentration camps or refugee camps, taken as a whole, are very much unhappier than other groups of people, and that that is what makes such institutions wrong?

The real snag in the utilitarian theory lies deeper than these difficulties of estimation. It was said that we know when one person is happier than another. But consider the religious ascetic face to face with a cheerful hedonist who is quite content with the available pleasures of life. Many people, judging by his expression and demeanour and comments, would say that the hedonist is happy. If we suppose him supplied with plenty of pleasures and no worries, who could be happier than such a man? But the ascetic would not agree. Such a life, he would say, is not happy at all. True happiness is quite different. It has nothing to do with the gratification of the senses and everything to do with the attunement of the soul to God. And while religious ascetics are nowadays rare, 'cultivated' or 'highly educated' people are not, and does not their judgment of the happiness of 'the masses' illustrate the same point? The masses may be happy playing bingo or listening to pops; but is not their alleged happiness, however lively, inferior in quality to that to be won from playing chess or listening to a fugue? There are indeed simple hedonists—we have all met them—who seem to be as satisfied as they could be; but are not the satisfactions of a Socrates to be preferred? The logical point lying behind these comments is obviously that 'happiness' is itself a value word, meaning roughly 'good state of satisfaction', and that there is considerable difference of opinion as to which satisfied states are good and which are not. People manifestly differ as to the further criteria that a satisfied state must meet in order to be good. The utilitarian, in fact, has been caught in the trap of trying to deduce a value from a fact. He wants to make our choice of values scientific by establishing a universally acceptable, because factual, procedure for accepting, rejecting, and applying them. The procedure consists in relating values to the happiness or unhappiness that results from their acceptance. But this assumes that both the presence or absence of happiness and the connection between it and the acceptance of the value are matters of fact. Now the connection may indeed be factual, though we have seen that there are difficulties in its estimation; but the presence or absence of happiness is plainly not. The 'uncultivated' pop-fan and the 'cultivated' intellectual differ profoundly in the satisfactions that they value; the experience that one calls happiness the other will dismiss as square or crude. And if, as with the inmates of a concentration camp, or with the transference of wealth from the very rich to the very poor, there are cases where almost everyone agrees about the happiness and unhappiness involved, that only means that it so happens that there are in fact some values (here the evil of extremes of pain, want, and necessity) about which almost everyone agrees, not that a way has been found of deciding what is valuable and what is not. In the last resort, therefore, the connection of our principles and ideals with the happiness or unhappiness to which their acceptance gives rise does not establish their alleged rationality. It only transfers our uncertainty from one place to another, from the question 'What is truly good?' to the question 'What is true happiness?'.

The religious and the liberal ideologists have failed to pass the test of reason. Can the Marxists do any better?

Marxists agree with utilitarians on two important preliminary points. They are as clear that the absolutists are wrong and that there can be no universal and necessary values; and they are no less clear that there must, instead, be some universal and necessary procedure for deciding scientifically what values must be deemed to hold at a given time. But they insist that the utilitarian appeal to happiness is useless; and the method that they recommend is of a very different kind.

The Marxist's argument against utilitarianism coincides at first with the one just used. It is superficial, he says, to think about conduct in terms of happiness, for happiness is of different kinds, according to the different nature of the human powers from whose successful exercise it springs. Human nature has developed in the course of history. The human capacities to act, think, imagine, create, organise, control, work, and feel have grown immensely in range, diversity, and power. Happiness springs from the full exercise of such powers as the individual has been able to develop; its value depends upon the quality of the powers from which it springs. We therefore obscure the issue if we think in terms of happiness; we must rather think in terms of human powers, and consequently in terms of the development of human powers. Our principles and ideals will be right and good in so far as acting upon them tends to develop and diversify still further the latent powers of man.

It is said that Indian villagers living only a few miles from a modern steel works will cling tenaciously to their ancient way of living, with all its abject poverty and squalor, rather than assimilate their lives to the new forces that are working near them. Let us suppose that that is true in India, as it certainly has often been true in the industrial revolutions of liberal Europe and socialist Russia; and let us also suppose that the people in question are so attached to their old world that if they were forced into the factories they would be and would remain unhappy. The utilitarian should presumably maintain that even if the villagers' labour force is needed they should not be compelled to give it. However eccentric it may seem to get happiness exclusively from this poverty-stricken way of life, if they do, they do; and if they are left to their own devices they will doubtless be able to instil those same attitudes into their children, so that one would have no grounds to interfere with their decisions now for the sake of the happiness of the next generation. But the

Marxist would dismiss this argument with contempt. The question is not, he says, what would make men happy, men being what they are, but rather what would develop further their physical, emotional, aesthetic, and intellectual powers, and so make human beings capable of happiness on a new scale. These villagers must suffer the upheavals of industrialisation in India, just as did their counterparts before them in England and in Russia. The price of human greatness must be paid. But what is the force of that 'must'? Why must the price of human greatness be paid in suffering? Ultimately, the Marxist argues, because the development of human powers cannot proceed smoothly. Each new development hardens with success into a class structure which it is the interest of the successful to maintain, and which they do maintain long after it has ceased to promote the further development of human life. But new development there must be in the end; the tide of human life cannot be dammed for ever; a break-through, a revolution, must occur; and some new class will ride the tide and pull their less-enter-prising neighbours, screaming and kicking, into the new epoch. All history is the history of revolution against the decaying remnants of the revolution before.

It is only against this background that values and the justification of values can be understood. The values current at any time belong either to the old epoch or to the new. Either they codify the way of life of those who made the last revolution, and are seeking to retain the advantages it gave them; or they foreshadow the way of life of those who are destined to break through that shell of old achievements into a new age of human power. And this view, evidently, has drastic consequences. For one thing, it strictly excludes the possibility—after which the other theories have aspired—of finding any argument that would bridge the gap between the old values and the new. Morality is class morality. You can argue within classes but not between them. Between them, in the nature of the case, there are no common pre-mises from which an argument could begin : that is precisely what is meant by calling human history revolutionary. Values formulate the aims and principles of social move-ments; the social movements are antithetical; therefore the values are antithetical. But inside the class that makes the movement and shares the assumptions of the movement argument is possible. And here Marxism makes its second point: the argument is of a special kind. Let us put ourselves on the revolutionary side. Since values only have significance in relation to the movement, it must be by their contribution to the movement that they are to be accepted or rejected. If the principle is conducive to the movement, yes; if not, no. It follows that one must know what is conducive to the movement and, therefore, what the movement is. But to know what the movement is involves placing it in the sweep of history; and that involves understanding what mankind is bringing forth, what stage in the process has been reached, what the old forces are that prevent the next development, what the new forces are that will notwithstanding drive it through, and how, in general, they will do so. To support values we must therefore have a thorough grasp of both the grand strategy of human liberation and the immediate tactical situation. As true revolutionaries we will then accept or reject values according to the effect that has upon the cause of liberation so defined; in the present epoch, the cause of the proletariat. As for our enemies, the forces of reaction, they will, of course, continue to assert their old morality, wrapping it up with every mystification of religion, intuition, and utility that may help to represent it as the morality of man in general, which it is not, rather than the morality of a diseased and dying social order, which it is. Indeed, the Marxist concludes, all this talk about supporting values is so much bourgeois mystification. It suggests, and is obviously intended to suggest, that values, like statements of history or physics, can be supported by argument; it suggests that values have a common ground, discoverable and acceptable by all men of reason and goodwill. But so long as class society exists that simply is not true. So long as there is systematic exploitation of one class by another, and the classless society is no more than an expectation for the future, so long will values be weapons of class war, and any pretence of rational argument about them will be no more than a subtle attempt to conceal the inevitability of revolution.

The Programme of the Soviet Communist Party, 1961, expresses this whole position as follows:

'In the course of transition to communism, the moral principles of society become increasingly important; the sphere of action of the moral factor expands and the importance of the administrative control of human relations diminishes accordingly. The Party will encourage all forms of conscious civic self-discipline leading to the assertion and promotion of the basic rules of the communist way of life.

'The Communists reject the class morality of the exploiters; in contrast to the perverse, selfish views, and morals of the old world, they promote communist morality, which is the noblest and most just morality, for it expresses the interests and ideals of the whole of working mankind. Communism makes the elementary standards of morality and justice, which were distorted or shamelessly flouted under the rule of the exploiters, inviolable rules for relations both between individuals and between peoples. Communist morality encompasses the fundamental norms of human morality which the masses of the people evolved in the course of millennia as they fought against vice and social oppression. The revolutionary morality of the working class is of particular importance to the moral advancement of society. As socialist and communist construction progresses, communist morality is enriched with new principles, a new content.

'The Party holds that *the moral code of the builder of communism* should comprise the following principles:

devotion to the communist cause; love of the socialist motherland and of the other socialist countries;

conscientious labour for the good of society—he who does not work, neither shall he eat;

concern on the part of everyone for the preservation and growth of public wealth;

a high sense of public duty; intolerance of actions harmful to the public interest;

collectivism and comradely mutual assistance; one for all and all for one; humane relations and mutual respect between individuals—man is to man a friend, comrade, and brother;

honesty and truthfulness, moral purity, modesty, and unpretentiousness in social and private life;

mutual respect in the family, and concern for the upbringing of children;

an uncompromising attitude to injustice, parasitism, dishonesty, careerism, and money-grubbing;

friendship and brotherhood among all peoples of the U.S.S.R.; intolerance of national and racial hatred;
    an uncompromising attitude to the enemies of communism, peace and the freedom of nations;
    fraternal solidarity with the working people of all countries, and with all peoples.'

Now both the substantial content of these rules and the precariousness of their foundations are concealed by the device that has already been analysed at length of using terms which have an evaluative content as if they were purely factual. It requires no elaborate train of reasoning to show that an uncompromising attitude to injustice, parasitism, dishonesty, careerism, and money-grubbing is a virtue, for all those terms, beside their factual content, bear a heavy load of disapproval; the so-called principle is really a tautology that reasserts, perhaps more emphatically, the values that have already been asserted by referring, for example, to a concern for one's own advancement as 'careerism' or 'money-grubbing'. But, still, there is a point of substance here, however misleadingly expressed. The Marxist would view with disgust the long sections of the British Sunday papers that give advice on how to enrich oneself by speculative investment. He would hold it a corruption, both of the individual who does it and of the society that permits and encourages it, to apply one's mind to securing for oneself a larger portion of the goods produced by one's fellows without helping to produce them. This, to the Marxist, is plain, cynical egoism; money-grubbing, in a word. Our problem concerns the nature of his reasons for maintaining such a value.

In the first place the Marxist is not opposed to profit-making as such. So long as the pursuit of gain effectively increases production, as it did in early capitalism, Marx viewed it benignly. His objection to profit-making is that, together with the whole method of organising production of which it forms a part, it has now come to act as a brake on the development of man's productive powers. The underlying pattern of the Marxist argument is therefore: whatever acts as a brake on production is wrong; profit-making does so act; profit-making must therefore be rejected and can properly be called 'money-grubbing'. Hidden within the argument we therefore find the familiar combination of a factual with a value premise; all we have done is to bring them to the surface. And now that we have got them there we could, of course, attack the value premise in exactly the same way that we have attacked value premises before. We could ask for its support, show that any support that it is given will involve further value assumptions from which other people may and will dissent, and conclude that this value is as irrational as any other. And in driving this argument home we need not be beguiled by the Marxist device of making 'human liberation' tacitly synonymous with 'increasing productive power'. To make such an identification is indeed the whole point of the materialist conception of history; but we, as canny logicians, cannot be a party to excluding by definition all other schemes of value—the scheme, for example, of the other-worldly ascetic.

This argument is perfectly conclusive, and with it we have brought to an end our examination of the ideologists' attempts to establish the concept of rational values, and to use it to reinforce the practical policies of the institutions to which they belong. We have seen that much of the power of ideological writings lies simply in the skilful use of the emotive power of words. We have also seen that that power is greatly reinforced by a certain appearance of objectivity which the ideologists assume. How much less effective would their writings be if they came to us, like advertisements, as open attempts to manipulate our actions! How persuasive is their air of scientific objectivity! But to that air the concept of value is essential; for a value is, by definition, a practical position which can be seen by common reason to be a common obligation. It is this concept that has now collapsed. When we examine the phrase 'seen by common reason to be a common obligation' we find that it means nothing. Values do not follow logically from facts. They can follow logically from one another; but unless that regression can be ended, the set of values that it brings together is as unfounded as the single value from which it began. The theologian then says that the set of values—*his* set of values, naturally—is founded on the authority of God; but he cannot tell us how God's commands can be rationally discovered. The intuitionist then says that the basic values are self-evident; but he cannot tell us how to decide rationally between our claim to self-evidence and its rivals. The utilitarians claim that values can be founded on their relationship to happiness, but they cannot say what reason is to do when people disagree as to what constitutes true happiness. The Marxist asserts that the valuable is whatever contributes to the current revolution. What we have said to this so far is that it can be flatly contradicted—by the Stoic or the Apostle, for instance—with just as much right, or as little, as it can be flatly asserted. But there is a further and equally interesting point. Even if we accepted for the sake of argument the Marxist's value premise that the right is what promotes, the wrong is what hampers, the growth of man's productive power, who is to say what promotes it and what hampers? The difficulty is not only that values vanish down a vicious spiral of interdependence into nothing; it is that the alleged facts on which the ideologists rely are highly dubious; and this is the next issue to be dealt with.

Meanwhile one piquant observation is in order. Each of our ideologists says of all the rest that their schemes of value are hypocritical moonshine, mere masks of objectivity to conceal the play of selfish purpose. The difference between us and them is that what each says of the rest we say of all. How pleasing for the sceptic, when he attacks the Marxist, the Catholic, or the American for their bogus rationalisations, to have the American, the Catholic, or the Marxist on his side !

6

Facts in Dispute

FOR the sake of argument let us continue to put aside our sinister conclusion that the distinction between values and personal attitudes, between 'that is good' and 'that is what I want', cannot be made on the basis that the former can be rationally justified, the latter not. In any case it is plain that there is *some* difference, even if not one of rationality, between them; and we shall eventually have to say what it is. But first we must examine another question: the character of the facts upon which values in general, and the value of freedom in particular, must depend. When it has become visible how grossly the ideologists simplify, distort, and embellish the facts of society and human nature, in order to adapt them to their cause, the role of values in their argumentation can be finally determined. What, then, are the facts of freedom?

We normally use 'free' to commend the absence of some restriction or other on some capacity to act. More than that is not involved in the meaning of the word, as meanings are reported in a dictionary. But plainly very much more is involved when the word is used on some particular occasion. When the released prisoner cries 'Free, at last!', when the doctor pronounces his patient free of a disease, or when the ascetic longs to be free from sin, they are all commending the absence of a restriction upon a capacity to act. But both the capacity and the restriction in question vary with the circumstances. The capacity may be that of locomotion, of leading an ordinary life, of command over passion, or a hundred others; the restriction may be prison walls, bacterial infection, the forces of desire, or others just as numerous: which capacity is in question, and which restrictions, are not laid down by the meaning of the word. Instead, they are generally made plain by the context in which the word is used. Thus in the context of release from prison no one who was acquainted with the circumstances would suppose that the ex-prisoner was commending the absence in himself of the restrictions imposed by passion or bacterial infection; his theme would be the absence of the restriction imposed by prison walls on his capacity to move around. This is another striking instance of the economy of language. It would be intolerably cumbrous to have a different word in the dictionary for every set of circumstances in which we wish to commend the absence of restrictions upon human activities; it is far more efficient to have one word for that general purpose and to let its specific import be supplied on each occasion by the particular context of its use. But, still, this powerful linguistic device gives rise to difficulties. It seems quite possible, for instance, that while the speaker may think that the context makes plain what particular freedom he has in mind, it actually does not. The hearer may collect no clear idea at all, or may collect the wrong one. Worse still, he may collect the wrong one without knowing that he has. Clearly, there is much scope here for confusion and misunderstanding, and an equal need for logical elucidation, if crossed argument is to be avoided.

What does 'context' mean? It means first the verbal context. If people have been talking about marriage and one of them then says 'but I still think that women should be free', the topic of the conversation makes it plain that he is thinking of some freedom of women from the authority or power of men. And if the immediate topic has been that of having children, the verbal context will make it clear, perhaps, that the freedom in question is that of practising contraception and so of having children if and when they please. The context, however, need not be verbal. If people have been looking at a film of life in an Arab village the freedom in question might obviously be that from heavy labour; if the people are Swiss and have been listening to election results the freedom might just as obviously be that to vote; in either case, without any direct verbal preparation. That being so, the possibilities both of economical understanding and of gross misunderstanding are very great. Consider further the case of the Arab village. Much will depend on what themes, precisely, the film has emphasised. Fetching water in heavy pots? Doing all the agricultural labour? Having multitudes of children? Being liable to unilateral divorce? Perhaps all these have been touched on; but while the speaker has been struck by one the hearer may have been struck by another. Or perhaps the speaker feels moved to condemn the whole situation without having thought out whether he condemns every part of it equally. In these and many other ways the parties to the discussion may easily be betrayed by the very efficiency of the word 'free' into misunderstanding what others, even what they themselves, have got in mind and wish to argue for. Thus there are as many freedoms as there are human capacities whose unrestrictedness someone or other wishes to commend; and which freedom is at issue on any occasion will depend upon the verbal and non-verbal context. But since the users of the word are often unclear which freedom it is they have in mind, and since, even when they are clear, the context may fail to convey that clarity to others, it can very well happen either that one or all parties to the debate have no definite idea of what they are debating, or that while their several ideas are definite, these, without their knowing it, are not the same.

From these considerations follows a further rule of logical hygiene in dealing with questions of freedom. We must not only keep tabs on our emotions and, realising that values are at stake, recognise the difficulty of giving values any agreed support; we must always bear in mind the need to make quite sure both that we know what it is on which we are setting a value, and that this is clear to the other parties to the discussion. Likewise, if someone else is advancing a case for freedom we must be sure that he makes clear what capacity to act he has in mind and what restriction upon it he wishes to condemn. In the useful everyday phrases, we must make sure both *for what* and *from what* freedom is being claimed. We cannot assume that the mere use of the word will establish these points. The dictionary meaning of the word does not reach them, but only begins a process of identification which the context should complete; and the context may, more or less completely, fail to do so. And while the importance of this simple rule of hygiene only becomes entirely clear when it is used on important examples, the following consideration shows where the wind is blowing: if the rule is not observed what would be more easy, more fatally easy, than to suppose that several different freedoms, just because they have not been carefully specified and therefore separated, are really one big freedom; and so for people to be led on to assume that because one of them can be achieved in a certain way the achievement of the others will follow automatically? And may not this be precisely what is happening when Marxists expect so much from the social control of the means of production, Catholics from moral obedience, Americans from the vote? But be that as it may turn out to be, the morals are clear. Always specify, or at least do your best to specify, the kind or kinds of freedom that you are seeking to commend! And always be prepared to find, when you have done so, that the freedoms you are after are not conveniently tied together, but are quite separate from each other, or, just as likely, stand in conflict! For life is a choice of freedoms. Freedom for men to choose what sexual partners they please from time to time conflicts with freedom from insecurity for mothers and children; freedom of entrepreneurs to invest as they see fit conflicts with the freedom of backward and commercially unattractive areas to develop their resources; freedom for philosophers to speculate conflicts with the freedom of the powers that be from the statement of inconvenient truths.

Suppose, then, that these morals have been noted and these rules observed. We therefore have at least a rough idea both *for what* and *from what* freedom is being claimed. We have begun to get a grip on the facts of the case. But can we count on that grip remaining secure? Unfortunately, we cannot. The kinds of fact involved when we are dealing with human actions are very slippery. In particular: the terms that are at our disposal for describing human conduct and human situations are very vague; conduct and situations vary widely through space and time; we cannot always use the experimental method to improve our knowledge; and while, in making up our minds on practical matters, what we need to know is the course of events that will follow upon this action or on that, the number of facts affecting the upshot of our actions is so vast, and usually so little understood, that rational predictions are hard to come by. The vagueness, variability, untestability, and multiplicity of the facts involved in practical thinking must be watched as carefully as the emotions and values of the thinker.

Factual or descriptive terms are those whose normal function is to refer to the properties that things possess and the relations in which they may stand to one another. Thus 'sweet', 'red', 'rectangular', 'magnetic', 'magnetisable', 'right-handed', 'excitable', 'father of', 'planet of', 'between' are all factual or descriptive terms. Let us now use the term descriptive for them rather than 'factual', since 'factual' suggests 'true' and these terms can just as well be used to state errors as to state what is the case. Moreover, these terms are, of course, not only used for making statements. If I promise to repay a debt, or express my regret that I have failed to do so, 'repay my debt' serves to describe the situation that I have promised, and regret having failed, to bring about. We therefore need a word to pick out the function of words in determining what a situation is like, what the properties and relations of the things involved are; and 'descriptive', though not ideal—for when we use descriptive words we are not usually in the everyday sense describing, that is, specifically setting ourselves to characterise—seems to be the best word for the purpose. And as for the distinction between properties and relations, it is both obscure in itself and of small importance for our present purposes. 'Sweet' seems to designate a property, but is it not a relation between a kind of substance and an organism? 'Father of' seems to designate a relation, but can it not be construed as a property of the father? Let us then leave it that we shall use 'property' when we think in terms of characterising a single thing, no doubt in artificial isolation, and 'relation' when we think in terms of simultaneously characterising more things than one. Our first concern is with a different aspect of descriptive terms: their vagueness or precision.

Our purpose in speaking and writing is usually to communicate—not always, since, even if we have a conscious purpose and are not, for example, just talking in our sleep, we may just be doing it to amuse ourselves. Our purpose in communicating is usually to convey something definite—not always, since, if we are gossips, our only object may be to hold our neighbour's attention to ourselves. The definite thing that we seek to convey may be of many different kinds. It may be a piece of information, an order, a promise, a desire, a submission, or whatever else. But whatever it is its definiteness will largely depend on the definiteness of the descriptive terms that it contains. It is indeed true that the form of words, taken by itself, may leave room for doubt as to what kind of communication it is. 'I hope you will finish that today' may just express a hope, but as said by the boss to an employee it amounts to a command. 'It will be there' may express a prediction, but if the object's being there depends upon the actions of the speaker it may rather express an undertaking. The context of utterance plays its part here, as it did in determining the relevant force of 'free'; and when it fails to do so unambiguously the prudent hearer demands from the speaker an explicit 'I just hope', 'I order', 'I predict', or 'I assure you'. It is plain that in arguing that 'free', besides simply conveying emotions, is used to express both attitudes and values, we have been drawing, precisely, a distinction of this kind. If a man says 'I'm free at last!' we need to know whether he is just saying how nice it is for some capacity of his to be impeded no longer, or whether he is claiming that that release is right. But we are supposing for the moment that any such ambiguity has been cleared up, and are therefore turning to consider the ambiguities and difficulties that arise from the descriptive content of such utterances rather than from their active form.

'Odd-numbered' is a descriptive word. If I know that a collection of objects is odd-numbered I know something about it, often something important. Now 'odd-numbered' is plainly a very precise term. It means one thing and one thing only, and there is a foolproof procedure for deciding whether it applies in a given case or not. Of course, if the objects that form the collection are very remote, very numerous, or very fluctuating, or if the collection itself is only vaguely defined—all of which would be true of the collection of molecules of water in a cloud—we cannot in fact say whether the collection is odd-numbered or not; but that is on account of practical difficulties and the vagueness of 'cloud', and implies no vagueness in 'odd-numbered'. Where such difficulties do not arise—as with the number of apples in a box before us—there can be no doubt about the application of the term. And the crucial test of this is the fact that different people can agree on the meaning of the term to such good effect that, practical difficulties, rectifiable mistakes, and ambiguity of other terms apart, they do always in practice agree

on whether a collection is odd-numbered or not. In the operation of pairing off we have a clear and complete procedure for
deciding the matter; and this procedure does in fact produce
consistent results both as between different observers and as
between different observations of the same observer.

The word 'hot', although equally a descriptive word, is,
by comparison, vague. In the first place it is simply ambiguous. There is hot temper, hot pace, and metaphorical
hot water as well as the hot water that one has in one's
bath; but let all the other meanings than that of temperature
be put aside. A day and a kettle of boiling water are both hot
in the same sense of the term, but a different range of tem-
peratures is implied by the use of it in the different cases;
here context enters again to determine what the relevant
range of temperature roughly is. But let us put that ambiguity aside and consider hot days only. We must then put
aside the ambiguity that arises from the fact that what
would be called a hot day in December or in London would
not be in June or in Singapore. But even when we restrict
ourselves to a day and place and season, different people
often disagree as to whether it is hot. If we simply go by
how we feel, differences in mood and health and constitution lead us to make a different judgment. As so defined—or,
rather, as so left undefined—the term is vague; and while,
of course, there will be frequent instances on whose hotness
everybody will agree, in spite of the peripheral vagueness of
the term, borderline cases will be frequent, close comparisons
of temperature will be impossible, and, in general, disagreements about its application will constantly arise.

Modern science is commonly associated with the elabora-
tion of imposing theories; and that is correct, since the
theories were of a new and potent kind. But in order for the
new theories to be potent in the understanding and control
of nature, another kind of work had to be done. The potency
of scientific theories is their power to enable us to make
precise predictions of events. Given precise predictions, we
can handle things precisely and make them do just what we
want. But the preciseness of predictions depends on the preciseness of the terms in which they are expressed. There can
be no precise predictions about the phenomena of heat, and
so no potent theory in this field, so long as we have to work
with a term as vague as 'hot'. If a theory implies that at a

certain time one body should be a little hotter than another, and we only have our skin to judge by, different people will report differently and the value of the theory will remain unknown. If we want potent theories we must therefore find ways of rendering more precise the terms in which we make and report our observations. We must contrive to keep differences of judgment inside certain definite limits. At the very least we must derive techniques for making precise comparisons of degree; ideally we should do still better and replace comparisons of degree with comparisons of quantity. For when we apply our concepts by counting rather than by judgment they acquire the same objectivity as the concept of odd-numberedness; moreover, when we have expressed the presence of a concept by a number, as we do when we measure a distance, a weight, a pressure, an interval of time, or an electric charge, we can express our statements about these things in mathematical form and so win for our study of nature all the order, generality, and rigour with which mathematics provide us. Measurement, the art of giving vague, qualitative concepts a precise, quantitative form, lies at the foundation of science; on it chiefly depends that settled agreement between observers about the application of concepts without which there can be no objective observation and so no useful theory. And measurement depends on the discovery of such regular connections between a qualitative concept, like heat, and a quantitative phenomenon, like the expansion and contraction of a column of mercury, that the latter can replace the former in all rigorous thinking. The history of science has thus been, amongst other things, the history of the invention of such techniques of measurement; laboratories are full of instruments of measurement which, though much more complex than a ruler, are, like it, the visible, manipulable forms of some abstract but precise idea.

The next difficulty in thinking about freedom can now be simply stated: the terms we have available with which to describe human capacities, their impediments and their results, are mostly very vague, and are likely to remain so. Thus one line of argument against arranged marriage is to point to the erotic dissatisfaction, if not worse, that is alleged to be caused by this way of making matches. Those who favour the institution will no doubt argue, on the other hand, that romantic marriage does little or no better in this respect; the experience of Western countries since divorce became easy certainly does not suggest that it is very successful. Contrary facts have therefore been alleged. Let us now suppose that all questions of the value of erotic satisfaction can be put aside and that neutral language has been found to describe the facts in question. That is more difficult than might be thought, for sexuality evokes powerful attitudes and values which soon colour and (in relation to our scientific purposes) distort whatever language we apply to it. However, let us suppose the job has been done, so that emotions, attitudes, and values are kept firmly on one side while the facts are considered. What chance is there of reaching agreement on the facts? The truth is that while individuals can make fairly good qualitative comparisons, in point of satisfaction, between recent erotic experiences, the quality of their experiences becomes so hazy with time and wishful thinking that the comparison soon becomes unreal; and when it comes to making comparisons between different individuals, still more between different groups of individuals, imagination boggles. By contrast, the effects of diet on health can be exactly assessed: we can measure the intake of the various elements of diet in various populations, and we can measure their weight, stature, and liability to disease. But nobody has the least idea how analogous measurements could be made for erotic satisfaction. Thus while, on the values of most of us, though not of all, erotic satisfaction is important in judging the value of a particular marriage or institution of marriage, we have to admit that the facts of erotic satisfaction are very hard to establish. We know enough to be able to condemn female circumcision on this ground alone; the operation is said to destroy all satisfaction whatever, and this fact can doubtless be determined with confidence. But where the factors influencing satisfaction are less radical, so that it is all a subtle matter of degree, and where the satisfactions of different people have to be put together without our being able to measure and add them, we seem to come to an impasse. A piece of knowledge essential to our thought about the emancipation of women is simply not available.

Another striking case is provided by the value of freedom of discussion. The prophets of liberty—in England notably Milton and Mill—have regularly maintained that freedom of discussion is essential to a vigorous, creative, intellectual life. Relying on the same principle, many recent writers have argued that Communist despotism must wither, since it is incompatible with the intellectual life that is beginning to flourish in Communist countries. Writers in this vein do not hesitate to appeal to facts, arguing that it is visibly the case that the mind withers under despotism. Other people have commented by pointing to various despotic societies—Renaissance Italy or the France of La Grande Époque—where intellectual life has flourished. Once again these facts, if they could only be established, would obviously be of great importance; once again it may just be possible to eliminate from words like 'despotism' and 'creative' any misleading emotive or evaluative force, so leaving the descriptive element bare. But even if this were possible could one hope to formulate a proposition precise enough to be definitely confirmed by experience and effectively used in prediction, and so in action? The varieties of authoritarian rule and intellectual originality are so enormous that it is almost impossible to conceive the achievement of that precision of meaning that enables us to assert a definite connection between, say, vaccination and freedom from smallpox. In fact, it is pretty certain that terms like 'arranged marriage', 'erotic satisfaction', 'authoritarian rule', and 'intellectual originality' are internally much too complex ever to be made precise as they stand. These terms, after all, are only the best that common sense and unsystematic speculation have so far been able to devise for the classification of extremely subtle data. They are little more than terms of ordinary language, and there is nothing sacred about ordinary language. On the contrary, whenever science gets going on an area of experience the intuitive classifications that have previously prevailed usually have to be radically altered. Before Newton the movements of planets and projectiles seemed, very naturally, to be of wholly different kinds; his achievement was to show that they exemplified the same laws. Before bacteriology, fevers were classified on principles that had nothing to do with their true nature. Obviously, with respect to mental states and capacities, we are at best in the state of physics before Newton, or of biology before Pasteur; alarmingly (for those who favour reason) fifty years if ubtebsuve effort to discover techniques for measuring intelligence have only met with moderate success. Many things no doubt get measured; but how they fit together into intelligence, and whether they cover everything covered by that term, remains in doubt. Thus, while we are certainly making some progress in our knowledge of the mind, the fact remains that our concepts of mental capacities and states, on whose precision rational thought about freedom must depend, are still extremely woolly, and are likely to remain so.

Ironically, our very concern for certain important kinds of freedom prolongs this unsatisfactory situation. We have been able to achieve a rational classification of infectious diseases not merely because the microscope, the thermometer, and other instruments have enabled us to describe their features with precision, but also because we have been free to experiment upon them. The value of health is so universally agreed, and the treatments of ill-health have, in general, so little effect upon the rest of personality, that sufferers have no objection to being the subjects of experimentation; it has therefore been possible to subject medical concepts and hypotheses to rigorous tests. Modern medicine is the result. Now there can be no doubt that if we could take people from birth and carefully subject them to all sorts of differential treatment we should rapidly get to know a lot more than we do about mental states and qualities. We may believe, for example, that there is a connection between authoritarian handling in childhood and adult over-conscientiousness, perhaps neurosis. But is that true? If we could take large batches of children and subject them to varieties of treatment carefully specified in point of authoritarianism (thereby breaking down that concept into precise elements), and then made a comparative study of their subsequent careers, we might begin to get somewhere. But to treat human beings in that way conflicts both with the freedom of parents to bring up their children and with the freedom of children to have whatever seems to us (however vaguely and ill-foundedly) the best upbringing and education. That being so, we have to get along as best we can with what data the world provides and which, not being standardised experimentally, is very hard to compare and interpret.

Moreover, even when we can get round the moral objection, other difficulties stand in the way of experimentation with human beings. The first is the fact that the people, being

conscious and intelligent animals, are liable to get wind of
the fact that they are being made the objects of experiment
and, for that very reason, to act differently. Their behaviour
is thus changed by the fact of experimentation. It is hard
to imagine any experimental set-up in which our children
would not at some point tumble to the fact that they were
being specially treated and would react to this knowledge—
at least later on when, as the experiment would require, they
went out and mixed in the world. The second is the fact
that even if neither moral principles nor the sensitivity of
human beings got in the way of experimentation, it seems
that human patterns of life are so intricately connected with
one another and so variable through time that it must remain
extremely difficult to isolate any reasonably simple regu-
larities of behaviour which can then be counted on to hold
in different circumstances. To take an example of immense
importance on any view of human freedom: industrialisation changes profoundly the conditions of life; in some ways
(on the values of most of us) it liberates—for example, from
heavy toil and bad diet; in other ways it restricts—through
the necessity it imposes of centralised social control, personal discipline, and regular routine. So much we can see.
But what is happening underneath the surface? It is obvious
that industrialised life is having profound effects upon every
side of human life: upon women (smaller families and
lighter work), upon children (more intensive education),
upon adolescents (earlier maturity, earlier psychological independence, prolonged education)—indeed upon every category of human being and every aspect of existence. Even
if we could arrive at an understanding of some of these factors, taken by themselves, we should still be in the difficulty
that they cannot be so taken because, in reality, they inter-act.

The various aspects of human life are not relatively
isolated by nature, like solar systems, and cannot be isolated
by artifice like the contents of a test-tube; therefore, they
cannot be studied in simplifying disconnection from other
things. And even if that difficulty could be overcome—and
the pile of 'even ifs' has now grown large—the yet more
devastating fact remains that our knowledge would still be
limited to the effects of industrialisation at its present stage
in which, to take one point only, most men are obliged to do
a full week's work. What will be the effects on human life

of the age of computers and automation when society will
be far more centralised than it is now and leisure has become
the rule? We do not know, and it is very difficult to see how
we ever could; for all our evidence must be drawn from past
and present states of society, which differ from the society
of the future in respects that are surely fundamental. Moreover, any views we may form on this or similar topics are
liable to have an influence upon society, and therefore to alter
the situation that they are meant to diagnose. Marxism has
transformed capitalism by making capitalists see better what
they must do if revolution is to be avoided. Theory, as much as
experiment, has effects upon its human subjects. The question
'Will industrialisation liberate, and, if so, in what respects?'
must, for this reason also, be extremely hazardous to answer.

The facts of human freedom are, therefore, very slippery
indeed. This freedom concerns human capacities to act and
feel. To establish or to contradict a claim to freedom we
must therefore be able to establish facts about capacities
and feelings. Our present language in this field is very vague;
'hot' is not good enough for physics, but 'intelligent' or
'satisfaction', which are typical of the concepts that we have
to use in thinking about freedom, are much woollier than
'hot'; for the feeling of temperature, however crude, is much
more efficient, as measured by the test of regular agreement,
than the estimation of a mental quality. Moreover, the key
procedure for making concepts more precise, systematic
experimentation, is largely denied us in the case of human
beings, first by our moral scruples, and then by their response to being the subjects of experimentation and of
theory. Finally, the various aspects of human life are in-
extricably intertwined, and vary through time. While therefore we often can establish facts that are relevant to freedom
—when one comes to think about it, the whole of medicine
can be seen as simply as that—often, and then with respect
to topics of such great importance as erotic satisfaction, or
intellectual originality, or authoritarian upbringing, or the
effects of automation, it is impossible to assert anything
precise in itself and well founded on experience.

That being so, one would expect the ideologists to be
cautious in thinking about freedom. One would expect them
to define with care the terms they use and to keep an eye
constantly open for the possibility that some unconsidered

vagueness is making them unsuitable for the work in hand. One would expect them to be always casting around for further evidence by which to confirm, qualify, or withdraw their statements. One would expect them to be alert to the possibility that completely untestable assertions will be masquerading in the guise of facts. One would expect them to keep constantly in view the immense diversity of freedoms that men pursue, and the complexity of the links between them. That is to say: one would expect these kinds of caution from anyone who had the least concern to establish rational understanding and co-operation with those whom he addresses. But what we find with the ideologists is exactly the reverse. With them, studious vagueness of terms, neglect of evidence, absurd oversimplification of causes and effects, and metaphysical obscurantism are the order of the day. In fact their logical conduct makes it perfectly clear that they are not in the least concerned with clarity and truth; they only want to put over a picture of the world that will condition people to act as they desire.

It would be unjust to criticise in detail on this score the five American Presidents whose speeches have been quoted, since they were talking as practical politicians, not as theorists. And we have in fact already criticised them, so far as that is legitimate, in considering their rhetorical use of the notion of the people's will. We saw that this notion is as false in point of fact as it is emotively effective. It is a brilliant device for giving people the exciting and encouraging impression that in voting, especially in voting for you, they are taking the great and right decisions for society at large; but nothing corresponds to this picture in reality. There we have only an immense multiplicity of conflicting and overlapping pressures and apathies working out in ways that are the decisions of no one in particular, though plainly in the interests of some. But this criticism of the democratic process has been made so fully by others that it would be pointless to repeat it here.

Nor is it necessary to spend much time on the Catholic. His contempt of fact is so glaring as to need no comment. His fundamental contention is that the ills of the world—chiefly, class conflict and war between states—can only be cured by the acceptance of certain truths, and that these truths can only be really accepted (understood, that is, and put into practice) under the guidance of the Church. Now if this were true there should plainly be some correlation between the power of the Church and the peacefulness of life, both within societies and between them. But, as everyone knows, the truth is exactly the reverse. In the economically advanced societies the end of class war is now in sight, but the period which has seen the beginning of that transformation has been precisely one in which religious life, and the influence of the Churches upon economic and social policy, has dwindled into insignificance. Or will the Catholic seriously maintain that class war is more in evidence in England, where the voice of his Church is weak, than in Spain or South America, where it is strong? As for war between states, the Cuban crisis was plainly a turning-point in history: does the Catholic seriously maintain that the peaceful outcome of that crisis was more the work of Kennedy, who was a member of his communion, than that of Khrushchev, who, for all his complete rejection of religion, had staked his entire political career on peaceful coexistence?

And underneath this contempt of particular facts there is systematic neglect of a general fact. Catholicism makes the tacit assumption that moral factors play the decisive part in history. The idea seems to be that to cure social evils it is both necessary and sufficient to convince people that is what they are. But the facts already mentioned show this idea to be naive. War within and between societies is not ending because men have suddenly become more virtuous; war is ending because it has become, with the change of circumstances, an obstacle to men's desires. In the dynamic industrial economy everyone can get more of what he wants without depriving his neighbour, but gets less in the long run if, by struggling with him, he slows the pace of the economy down; in the atomic age nobody gains and everybody loses by recourse to arms. Thus the moralistic approach of the Catholic Church to social problems is as unreal in principle as it is in detail, and must be seen to be so by anyone who looks without prejudice at the world around him.

But looking at the world without prejudice is not the Catholic's aim. He wishes to establish in our heads a picture of the world that will exert a certain influence upon our actions, and he is prepared to spin the facts around in any way that helps this purpose. Still worse, he is prepared to spin around the concept of fact itself. For it would be a travesty of Catholic social theory that concentrated on its moral views; the heart is the theology; and the heart of theology lies in treating assertions about God, with all their practical and emotional implications, as statements of fact. That God exists, that he created the world, that he laid down certain rules for man, his creatures, to obey: these contentions are said to be true, if not exactly in the same sense, yet also not wholly in a different sense to that in which it is true that Picasso exists and created *Guernica*. Integral to Christianity is the claim that its articles of faith are truths about the world, not edifying myths. But this claim contradicts itself. Suppose that having told you that Picasso created *Guernica* I first prove unable to tell you anything whatever about Picasso that would let you identify him amongst the other contents of the world, and then prove unable to explain in any way at all the meaning of 'create': then you would say that I did not know what I was talking about, and that though I was using English words, had in effect said nothing. But this is precisely the situation of the theologian. 'Create' in 'God created the world' cannot bear any of the meanings that it bears in ordinary life; for, if it did, God (like the Greek gods) would be just a part of nature, and not a possible object of Christian worship. 'God created the world' would become an empirical hypothesis, falsifiable in principle, and falsified in fact, by observation; while, for Christian faith, God's existence must be independent of nature and must be unquestionable, whatever happens. But if 'create' does not bear its ordinary meaning here it must be given another; and that is what the theologian cannot do; for the crux of his position is that God's relation to the world is unique, and cannot be explained in terms of any other. 'Create', therefore, is neither being used with any of its ordinary meanings, nor being endowed with a new one; and the same is true of all the other terms—like 'love' or 'knowledge'—by which God is supposed to be characterised. God is said to love the world he sustains, no matter what horrors happen by his leave; but if love is thus compatible with absolutely everything it has become absolutely nothing. So used, 'love', like 'create', is vacuous. But if these terms are vacuous the theologian cannot tell me how to identify the entity to which he purports to refer by the use of the word 'God'; he can neither point him out nor describe him to me, as we have seen he must be able to do, if his expression is to convey a genuine factual statement. It follows that the expression 'God created the world', while it obeys the rules of English grammar, does not fulfil the further logical conditions under which alone it can serve to express a statement of fact. It looks like such a statement, but is really nothing of the kind.

To put the point in a nutshell: the Catholic, like all theologians, is guilty of a profound equivocation. He wants his expressions to rank as statements that give information about the world, since otherwise they would lose the authoritativeness of fact and degenerate into myths and stories; but at the same time he cannot let them satisfy the conditions under which alone our experience can claim to express facts; for if these conditions were satisfied God would become at best a part of nature, and his existence would be a hypothesis to be used or discarded like any other. But with this conclusion, religious ideology, logically speaking, is reduced to nothing. It is not merely that even if God's existence is granted for the sake of argument, his existence in no way demands one set of values and excludes all others, though that is true; it is rather that the granting of God's existence is, logically speaking, a meaningless gesture. But if it is meaningless logically, emotively it is pregnant with practical significance. If, bemused by equivocation, we allow ourselves to think in terms of a supreme being whose will is made known to us by his terrestrial representatives, then the power of those representatives, and of the institutions to which they belong, is notably increased. The very logical defects become rhetorical advantages. If, without grasping the absurdity of the procedure, I both put God outside the world, by making him absolute, omnipotent, and mysterious, and also bring him into the world, as the sponsor of a particular social order, then that order will seem to be invested with all the mysterious authority attributed to God. And, to be fair to Catholics, this procedure is just as absurd when the beneficiary is the individual conscience rather than a Church. When a man has got himself to believe that the voice of conscience is the voice of God he has put himself outside the pale of rational discussion; he has in fact invented a story which makes it unnecessary for him to attend to the interests, or to listen to the criticisms, of his

neighbours; he has entitled himself to act on any forceful feelings he may have, as the priest has entitled himself to act on
any ecclesiastical interest. And that is the simple truth that
lies behind the convolutions of religious doctrine.

These logical flaws and persuasive powers of religious
utterances are tolerably familiar. They were, for example,
largely known to Marx, and their present familiarity owes
much to him. Less well known is the fact that Marx's own
chief assertions turn out to have exactly the same flaw, and
to derive from it the same persuasive advantage.

At first sight it seems absurd to accuse Marx of these
logical mistakes. He took sides passionately with science
against metaphysics. He claimed to see nature as science
progressively reveals it to us, neither more nor less. Man
arises out of nature and must be seen as a part of nature; the
evolution of society is part of evolution in general. And if
the theoretical problems of man are solved by placing him
in his natural position, the practical problems of deciding
what to do are solved by considering what his evolution next
necessitates. There is no vagueness here, it seems, no appeal
to abstract first principles or supersensible entities : just the
scientific study of things as they have been, as they are, and
as they must become. But when we get down into the detail
of Marx's theories this appearance of simplicity turns out to
be delusive. Marx is not a religious metaphysician, certainly;
but he is a social metaphysician instead.

The key concept of Marx's social theory is that of the proletariat, the class of wage-earners in capitalist society. When
we look backwards the proletariat is just the last in the long
succession of exploited and oppressed classes, wage-slaves
instead of serfs or slaves in the juridical sense. But when we
look forward the proletariat is unlike all previous oppressed
majorities, for it has not only the impulse but the power to
end oppression. The proletariat has the impulse because it is
an inherent necessity of capitalism to turn more and more
people into proletarians, and then to exploit them more and
more severely, until the bursting-point is reached; and the
proletariat has the power because it is an inherent necessity
of capitalism not only to create means of production so
efficient that one class no longer need exploit another, but
also to do so by gathering its workers into towns and factories where they naturally acquire the skills of co-operation

and revolution. And so all the suffering as well as all the creativity of man is brought together in the proletariat, which then, in one great heave, will throw off all the old shackles of class society and inaugurate an age of freedom. Thus the term 'proletariat' is given meaning by Marx in two quite separate ways. On the one hand it is defined, empirically, as the class of urban wage-workers in capitalist society; on the other hand it is defined, theoretically, as the class which is to raise mankind out of an oppressed into a free existence. Marxism asserts that this double definition is justified because the two descriptions coincide: the industrial wage-workers are to liberate mankind. But how do Marxists handle this assertion? When the double definition comes under strain, what do they do? Do they, as they would if their approach were really scientific, hold on to the empirical meaning of 'proletariat' and, when it appears that the industrial wage-worker is not behaving as a Marxist proletarian should, admit that their theory is now questionable? Or do they hold on at all costs to the theory of the liberating proletariat, and twist the stubborn facts to fit it?

It is not easy to say what Marx himself would have done had he lived till now, when capitalism has developed in an entirely different way from that which he predicted. In his own time the theory was not unreasonable. The condition of the working class was terrible; as crisis succeeded crisis he and Engels were not the only ones to think that the hour of revolution must soon come; and though things were changing in the last part of his life, it would not have been easy to discern that the inherent necessities of capitalism demanded the educated, orderly, well-to-do workers of the present day, instead of the oppressed masses of his theory, or that the state would come to play the main part in this transformation. Since Marx and Engels attacked dogmatic presentations of their views, it is nice to think that if they were living now in Western Europe or North America they would abandon the hypothesis that industrial workers would ever, in any significant sense, play the revolutionary, liberating role that they had been assigned. But while what Marx and Engels would have done is pure speculation, what Marxists have done is plain fact. Is it pointed out that the workers are getting richer, not poorer? They answer that while this may be true in absolute terms, the worker's share of the national income, relatively to that of the bourgeoisie, is getting smaller. Is it pointed out that the workers are no longer brutally oppressed, and that in Sweden and the United States the blue-collared workers are already outnumbered by the white? Then it is answered that they are still workers, since they do not own the means of production, and are being oppressed in subtler ways instead. Is it pointed out that Communist revolutions have only occurred in peasant countries? Then the word 'proletariat' is discreetly dropped and we hear only of 'toilers' or of 'workers and peasants'. Is it pointed out that the main Communist parties can therefore in no significant sense be said to be vanguards of the revolutionary proletariat created by industrialisation, but are instead the means by which economically backward countries are being industrialised? Then we are told that the economically backward countries were the 'weakest links' of international capitalism because, whether colonies or not, they were the most ruthlessly exploited by it, and that the Communist parties, securing their bases first in Russia and China, were acting for the movement of the working classes as a whole. These are typical Marxist explanations of how the theory is supposed to fit the modern world: what is to be made of them?

Marx's most general contentions about industrial society are obviously correct. The immense range of activities that even the most conservative of modern states has had to engage in proves that there is a contradiction between private property and the resources of modern society; and the power that urban workers have acquired by means of trade unions has been largely responsible for making the state act. But the theory breaks down over the nature of the workers' influence, which has been reformist, not revolutionary; over the adaptability of capitalism, which has proved to be compatible with full employment and rising standards of living; and over the development of poor countries, for which purpose a Marxist Party, dedicated to assert the power of man over nature as the essential condition for human liberation, has shown itself to be an effective instrument. Indeed, this cult of Promethean man has been so effective that it has completely eclipsed the empirical content of the theory. What does it matter if there is nothing in the world that corresponds to Marx's proletariat, provided that there is a widespread aspiration to achieve and enjoy material power, and to throw off the colonial yoke? All that has to be done is to replace the term 'proletariat' with a vague term like 'worker', and to call all those who feel that aspiration 'workers': then the whole Marxist doctrine of human liberation can be attached to the stumblings of mankind on the threshold of industrialisation and can be used to justify every brutality and rigour of Communist policy by 'proving' that it is a necessary step towards the golden age of the classless society.

But while this device is understandably effective in persuading people to follow a Communist Party line, it is fatal to the claims of any such line to be uniquely rational. Given the Marxist value premise that the right is what promotes, the wrong what hampers, the growth of man's productive power, everything then turns on the possibility of deciding rationally what really does promote and what really does hamper it; and on this the Marxist contention is that although no universally valid answer can be given, there is a universally valid procedure for finding the answer in any given case. There is, it is alleged, a science of social development, and Marxism is this science. The sequence of human liberation can be scientifically determined, and Marxism is supposed to do just that. But what we find in fact is precisely the reverse. In a science of human liberation, if there can be such a thing, the kinds of liberation should be precisely specified and the general principles for bringing them about should be clearly set out and scrupulously examined in the light of facts. On such an objective though tentative basis social policy could be the subject of rational discussion on the part of all concerned. But what we have in fact is a body of men—the party leaders—identifying themselves with the hero's role in a social myth—the myth of the liberating proletariat—and then constructing whatever 'facts' are needed to make the myth seem to fit the actual world.

In one of those candid moments which were the only endearing feature of Nazi life, General Goering said of the application of his racial principles: 'Who is a Jew is for me to decide.' Less candidly, but no less plainly, when all the wrappings of doctrine have been removed, we can hear our ideologists declaring: 'What God wills is for me to decide'; 'What history requires is for me to decide'; 'What intuition reveals is for me to decide.'

7

Necessity

A BODY falling downwards unimpeded by anything except the resistance of the air is said to fall freely. A jammed self-starter pinion, when it can move again along its shaft, may be said to have been freed; animals, no less than men, when released from trap or cage, are free again, even though they cannot say so for themselves. So what distinguishes human freedom from the freedoms of inanimate objects and of animals?

When we are dealing with the ability of inanimate objects to move and change the word 'free' tends to lose its emotive and evaluative force. No attitudes are implied when a body is described as falling freely; the only kind of meaning that remains is the descriptive one of absence of impediment. But in the case of the pinion an attitude seems to be expressed. We have a use for self-starters as not, in general, for falling bodies; and in order for them to do the work we want of them their pinions must be able to move along the shaft that connects them with the flywheel of the engine when the motor is switched on or off. We therefore have a favourable attitude towards pinions that can move; 'free' expresses that attitude when applied to a pinion that can now do so, just as 'jammed' previously expressed its opposite. By contrast we say that a car wheel that wobbles is not free but loose, and that a nut that is screwed down properly is tight. In all such cases it is some reference to constant human purposes served by the object that makes it normal for the words used in describing its state or performance to express an attitude at the same time. Nothing is implied about the purposes of the object itself, for this kind of object has no purposes at all.

'Free' can equally be used of animals, and even of people,

in just this way. A farmer who has been digging his sheep out of a snowdrift can say that he has freed them without implying anything more than that he has got them into a situation that suits him better than that in which they were; a conqueror who has removed a region from the power of a rival could use the same idiom and, conceivably, mean no more by it. He, like the mechanic with the pinion and the farmer with the sheep, would mean that he had freed them for his own purposes, which he naturally assumes to be good. He would realise, of course, that they have purposes of their own, and, if we changed the example, we could suppose that 'free' was intended to have some reference to them. But it need not do so. We can think about people, equally with sheep and pinions, as the instruments of our designs; we can call them free, irrespective of their own purposes, when some obstacle has been removed that prevented them with fitting in with what we want to do.

We never seriously attribute purposes to pinions, although in moments of frustration we may swear at them; we do not rate sheep much higher, as witness the force of 'sheeplike'. But the lover of wild life who frees a rabbit from a snare, or a gull of the oil on its feathers, almost certainly conceives himself to be freeing them for their purposes rather than for his own. He has, indeed, no other purpose than that of enabling them to go their own ways. How he thinks of their purposes is another matter; how he should think of them another still. Almost certainly he conceives the animals as disliking their situation; he may even go so far as to suppose that they disapprove of it; some people certainly suppose this with dogs and horses, if not with rabbits and gulls. And while this supposition of disapproval is almost certainly mistaken, the supposition of dislike is almost as certainly correct. It has even been suggested lately that flies have a rudimentary experience of pleasure, if not of pain. But if mammals know pleasure and pain in ways quite like our own it seems reasonable to say that their elaborate behaviour-patterns of seeking and avoidance manifest their attitudes towards things; and while they have not got our linguistic means of expressing their attitudes, no one who has lived closely with animals can fail to believe that they have others of their own. Dogs plainly show expectation, affection, gratitude, and grief. But if all that is true, then, when we let loose a dog who has

been tied up all day and say that he is free, although he is
then no more useful to us than before, the point of the
word must lie in the postulated feelings of the dog. We like
and approve the absence of the restriction of the leash upon
a dog's capacity to move around not just because it suits us
but because it suits the dog. Our use of 'free' signifies the
value we set on the exercise of the dog's capacities for their
own sake, not just for ours; and our setting this value on
them presupposes that they mean something to the dog. But,
of course, these two kinds of evaluation do not exclude each
other. If the dog is a working dog, then in calling him free,
because unleashed, I can simultaneously approve his being
able, as he moves around, both to work for me and to enjoy
himself.

This distinction, important to our thought about animals,
is crucial to our thought about human beings. The case of the
conqueror was somewhat artificial. It is strange to use 'free'
to characterise the situation of people being released from
impediments which are judged undesirable merely in relation
to the speaker's purposes, without regard for theirs. The
liberating conqueror has usually at least professed, however
hypocritically, to be freeing people for their sake, and only
indirectly for his own; in the typical case, that is what 'free'
implies. Human beings, still more than animals, have certain
powers of whose exercise we approve, although we may also
find it advantageous; when we talk of a characteristically
human freedom, a freedom peculiar to human beings, we are
referring with approval to these powers. What, then, are
they?

The first set are our powers of deliberate action. Given a
suitable upbringing most human beings develop to a greater
or lesser degree the capacity to interrupt the blind or intuitive flow of stimulus and response by such questions
(which need not be put in words, or, anyway, into so many
words) as : What am I doing? What will happen if I do that?
Is that what I really want? Should I? And besides these
powers of hesitating in the flow of action and wondering
what to do, human beings also come to possess the counter-
part powers of planning, deciding, executing, reconsidering.
With the infant in the cradle these powers have not yet
developed; with the mentally deficient they never have and

never will; under the influence of injury, fatigue, or intoxication they lapse for a time; in schizophrenia they lapse for
longer, perhaps indefinitely; in senility they have gone for
good. And with these powers of deliberate action others are
connected. All scientific thinking is implicit in the simple
practical question: What will happen if I do that? All art is
implicit in the style with which I do it. The distinctive
human power is the power of conscious origination in action,
thought, and fancy, with all that goes with it by way of
feelings, social relations, and material means of life. At
least, this is the power that strikes us men as being most
characteristic of ourselves, distinguishing us from any other
kind of creature with which we are acquainted; and it is to
the exercise of this power, in all its forms, that most of us
attach the highest value. If we imagine a nuclear holocaust
by which our race was destroyed we are horrified indeed at
the thought of the suffering it would entail, especially if we
imagine those we love to be involved; but what shocks us
still more deeply is the thought that human creativity would
have vanished from the earth. Hence, when we are obliged
to think about actual or imagined impediments to the exercise of this deepest human power we need a way of expressing our condemnation of them and our faith in its untram-
melled excellence, and 'freedom' or 'liberty', more precisely
and emphatically 'human freedom' or 'human liberty', are
the words we use. But the judgment that creativity is the
most excellent power of all, however certain we may think
of it, is still a value judgment; it is just one of the many
value judgments that we can make by means of 'free'. In
this case, as in the case of the released prisoner or the eman-
cipated woman, we are commending the absence of some
restriction upon the exercise of an approved capacity for
action. The fact that this capacity for origination exists, is
valued highly, and is implied in the value of other capacities
—the prisoner's purposeful walking off, the woman's purposeful voting—does not give 'free' here a different logic. All
the difficulties about values, which the ideologists proved
unable to resolve, crowd in upon us once again; but now a
new one follows on their heels.

What we have so far met are the difficulties of providing
rational support for our beliefs about freedom. Such support
is obviously needed if all the high-flown talk about ideals and

principles is not to be dismissed as mere hypocrisy; but the obscurities surrounding the justification of human values and the demonstration of human facts are such that it is not easy to see how it can be given. However, let us suppose it can. Let us take it for the moment that we have reached agreement as to what constitutes a rational argument on behalf of a value and that, on this occasion, the conditions have been met. Suppose now that the human capacity whose unrestrictedness is being commended is or involves the distinctively human capacity of origination. Suppose, for example, that it is a question of a people's right to choose its rulers by election, and that a country where they have this right is commended as being free; or suppose that an English girl speaks up for English customs, by comparison with those of other countries, by saying that she and her friends are free to choose their husbands; or suppose that the position of artists and philosophers in Communist countries is condemned by a liberal who contends that freedom is denied them. In each case some kind of choice or decision or conscious activity is being said to be free. But it seems that to say that a choice is free is to say that it could have been made in more than one way; for if it could only be made as it was made, then it would strictly be unavoidable, and so not free. But what does it mean to say that a choice can be made in more than one way? Presumably, that everything else inside or outside the agent can be just what it is, right up to the moment of choice, and yet the choice be different; for unless that is so, a real choice cannot be said to have been made. It seems then that when we apply the word 'free' to conscious activity, in which some kind of choice is always involved, we assume that at each moment of choice there is more than one genuinely open possibility that could be chosen, whether or not it was. Of course, when we used 'free' to commend, for example, the absence of disease, there is no such implication. We are saying that the person is free to do all sorts of things from which the disease prevented him; but the unimpeded activities need not involve choice, and so the present problem need not arise. But where the restrictions are not on the purely physical powers of the organism, but rather on the distinctively human powers of creative activity, predicating freedom seems to imply choice, and choice implies a genuinely open future. This is the thesis known as 'libertarianism'.

Why then should the future not be open, in this sense? What is wrong with the implication that it is? Just this: that when fully stated the thesis seems absurd, and that such little sense as can be given to it makes choice less comprehensible than ever.

Supposing that a choice is made by someone at a certain moment; for example, that a girl says 'Yes' to a suitor. Then the libertarian theory as to what is implied by specifically human freedom is that everything in the history of the universe could have been exactly what it was up to that moment, and yet a different choice could have been made: the girl could have said 'No'. Now that implies that something can happen—her saying 'Yes'—that is in no sense determined by what has gone before; and that surely is absurd. It is tantamount to the absurdity that events can occur in the universe that are not parts of the universe. There is no difficulty about events occurring whose connection with what went before escapes us; that is what we mean by chance. But the libertarian thesis maintains that in the case of choices there really is no such connection, not that we happen to be unaware of it; and that seems inconsistent with the very idea of an event.

Moreover, even if that were not so, the libertarian thesis seems to make incomprehensible precisely what it is supposed to explain: choice. Unless the girl's 'Yes' arises out of her character and situation, even though neither she nor we can see exactly how, what sense does it make to say that the choice was hers? Our choices, of all kinds, are our choices; they spring from our characters as so far formed and the situations in which we find ourselves; every time we take blame or credit for what we have done, every time we set ourselves to do better on the next occasion, every time we encourage one another or give advice, we acknowledge the truth of that elementary observation. Nothing that can be called a choice can be causally disconnected from our past; it must, on the contrary, be determined by it. Consequently, the future cannot be open, as the libertarian thesis requires. Whatever answer the girl gave was the answer, then and there, that had to be given.

That reply seems irresistible; but even if it is, the problem raised by libertarians remains. All the specifically human freedoms imply some kind of choice: how, then, is choice to be lodged inside the necessary sequence of events that constitutes the world? The freedom of the pinion can certainly be understood as part of the necessary causal sequences of nature; the freedom of the dog perhaps: but the freedom of the girl?

Now whatever the solution of this problem may be, one thing is certain: our systematic ideologists cannot provide it. American democracy is not systematic enough even to raise the question; but Marxism and Catholicism, which are, both raise it—and are bound to do so—in a way that involves them in hopeless contradiction. In their attempt to make the set of values that they favour absolutely solid, each system tries to lock them into a universal scheme of things in such a way that they can say: the world being what it is, this is how men must act. Now 'must', in that last phrase, is obviously ambiguous. It may mean 'should' or it may mean 'have to'; what is asserted by it may be either the obligation or else the necessity to act in certain ways. It is in the first of these senses that the ideologists appear to be taking the word. They are trying to make us adopt their way of life by proving that it is how we ought to live. But the very same reasoning by which they try to prove that we ought to live in such-and-such a way simultaneously proves that we cannot live in any way but that in which we do. The must of obligation dissolves into the must of necessity; man becomes a mere creature of forces external to his will.

How this happens in the Catholic—more generally in the Christian—case is now so old a story that it hardly bears retelling. The theologian objectifies morality by making it the law of God. But what must God be, if morality is to be his law for man? How must I think of God if calling morality his law is to make it objectively and absolutely binding on me? What must God know about me in order that his perceptions for us should not be open to question by me? Plainly he must know everything about my nature and the nature of the world in which I live; for if he did not, then some situation might arise for which his legislation would be inappropriate. Absolute legislation presupposes an exhaustive knowledge of the possible situations for which the

law is made. But such an exhaustive knowledge of the possibilities for a man implies exhaustive knowledge both of his
actual situation at each point of time and of the scientific
laws according to which his situation changes from one
point of time into the next. God cannot be an absolute legis-
lator unless he is presumed to know what the present is and
what the future must be. But if God knows what the future
must be, then our choices, which can only be properly so
called if they are open, are really closed before ever they are
made; and if they have been closed before they are made it is
absurd to tell us that we ought to make them in one way
rather than another. Legislation presupposes choice in those
for whom the laws are made; omniscience excludes it. To
legislate absolutely God must be omniscient; but if he is
omniscient he cannot legislate at all. The theory of divine
law is therefore absurd not only as an analysis of human
values, there being no way of telling which laws are divine,
but also as a theory of choice, there being no possibility of
choice at all on the assumptions that it makes as to how
choices should be guided.

To this simple argument the theologians of two millennia
have failed to find a satisfactory answer. All they do is to
continue to assert *both* that God knows everything *and* that
man is free to choose *and* that any seeming contradiction
between those propositions is due to the weakness of our
understandings. But that is a hypocritical evasion. Whenever
contradiction is no longer held to destroy a theory, the
common search for truth has ended and mere calculating
deception has begun.

Marx's contributions on this point are more subtle than
the theologian's. They are also, in virtue of their close affinity
with scientific modes of thought and speech, more influential.

One of Marx's main concerns was to show the effect of
social systems on the ways in which men think and act. In
particular he was interested in the effects exerted upon
thought and action of a particular kind of social system,
class society. This form of society, lasting from the dissolu-
tion of the tribe to the Communist society of the future, is
marked by the radical division of men into two groups, the
few who own and control the means of production, deriving
from that power all the advantages of wealth and culture,
and the many who do not. He claimed that any such society

is inherently unstable: men, in the nature of the case, must always struggle to escape from it. And he claimed that while scientific knowledge proper—knowledge, that is to say, that is based on observable fact and is therefore independent of social prejudice—has always existed even in the most class-ridden societies, most of what has passed for social knowledge in such societies has been the mere reflection of their inherent instability and has had no objective validity at all. All other forms of thought were twisted to consolidate the unstable interests of the ruling class. History was a mere mythical representation of their triumphs and their indispensability; the vast majority of the population, the workers, were not mentioned, or were only mentioned as drudges, menials, or victims. Religion was the opium of this driven mass of people. The principles of law were just the interests of their exploiters masked with the trappings of eternal justice. The philosopher's speculative concern with ideals, with spirit, and with absolute truth was just one long half-conscious obfuscation of the material needs of man. Marx did not say that this thinking was necessarily hypocritical, although he thought it often was. Priests, lawyers, and philosophers are the first to be deceived by their constructions, but deceived they are. Their systems have no objective validity; they only have a social role. But now that the age of class society is drawing to a close it has become relatively easy for the thinking man to free his mind from their spurious claims and to see them merely as social causes and effects. What used to be thought of as objective knowledge, the product of independent human reason, must now be thought of as mere links in the chain of social development. Men's theories, like their actions, arise necessarily out of what has gone before; the only specifically human freedom is that of grasping this necessity. But just because we can now conceive a human existence free of any exploitation as the practical possibility of the immediate future, it is no longer necessary for us to tell ourselves comforting fairy stories—such as Christianity—instead of looking at the facts. Now, for the first time, we can see ourselves as we really are; the inevitable process of human development can take place by our true understanding, rather than by our mythical distortion, of its nature; in so far as it does so, man is free.

Freedom is the consciousness of the necessity of the grand

historical process to which we belong. The values of our age are simply one of the forms that that necessity assumes as it unfolds into the endless future.

Superficially this view of human freedom is quite unlike the theologian's; in fact it descends directly from it and ends up in the same absurdity. The intermediary was Hegel. Hegel thought that Christian theologians were right in believing that the world is ultimately spiritual, that all history is providentially ordained, and that values are just one part of the providential ordinance; he thought that they were wrong in believing that values were permanent rather than historical, and that the scheme of Providence must remain a divine mystery, veiled from human eyes. Exactly the reverse was true: the scheme of Providence, the inevitable advance of man, could be laid bare by reason, and that was what he, Hegel, had achieved. Freedom was to be won through philosophical insight, like his own, into the necessity that makes us what we are. Brought up an Hegelian, Marx took over all these ideas, the spirituality apart. He too believed in a scheme of history, perfecting mankind step by step; he too believed that the rational necessity of that historical scheme could now be seen by men, and that that vision was the beginning of their liberation. But for Marx it was only the beginning. Just as he thought that the ultimate reality was material, not spiritual, so he thought that men must find their freedom through social action on the physical world, and not in rational contemplation merely. It was not enough to be a philosopher; one must be a practical revolutionary. Freedom is consciousness of necessity indeed; but it is only in social action that we can become fully conscious of the necessity by which we are impelled, fully free from the bonds of ignorance.

This mysterious doctrine may seem attractive in moments of conceptual intoxication, but coolly considered it in no way lessens the absurdity in which, together with the theologian, Marx is involved. In the attempt to make human action logically solid, he too has locked it into a sequence of events extending far beyond itself and determining its every detail. What men value, seek, and do is what they must, because they have been what they have been and are what they are. But if they must, then there is no more room for choice within the dialectic of matter than within the

providence of God; to make choice logically secure, in
either idiom, is to make it logically impossible; and to explain the contradiction away by saying that freedom is the
consciousness of necessity is just a verbal trick. Here, no less
than with the 'reconciliation' of free-will with Providence,
calculating deception has replaced the search for truth.

But what conclusions are we sceptical enquirers into
ideology to draw from the existence of these fatal contradictions? It seems plain enough that while one may object
to many details of Marx's theories about the determination
of men's thoughts and actions, nobody can now deny his
general thesis, nor many of his particular conclusions. It is
certain that the accounts that men have given of themselves
have been largely mythical, and that the particular nature
of these myths has been socially determined. Even the least
Marxist of historians nowadays declines to take at their face
value the accounts that political and religious movements
have given of themselves; they tend rather to explain them
as the consequences of social and economic movements
whose nature was unrecognised by the individuals who took
part in them; and even the least Marxist social psychologist,
faced by the problem of racialism and racial ideology, tends
to explain it in terms of the effects of a certain type of social
situation on a certain type of temperament. Thus it is
argued that the extreme insecurity of a social class breeds
aggressiveness; aggressiveness, to be acceptable to conscience,
requires an external evil to attack; when the real evil cannot
be attacked, a mythical evil must therefore be invented, and
those who are most insecure, for whatever reason, will do the
inventing. To take the most notorious example: the German
middle class in the twenties had been made very insecure by
war and inflation. The army and the banks could not be
challenged by a class who feared the proletariat. An enemy
had therefore to be invented: the evil Jew. Someone had
therefore to invent him: and so a man like Hitler, who,
given his personal background, would have been insecure
but harmless in a more stable society, could take the lead.

This last sort of theory is eclectic. In order to fit such a
phenomenon as Nazism into the web of causes and effects
it draws on Freudian theories of the origins of feelings as
well as on Marxist theories of class conflict. But, whatever

the theories, their use and their success is plain. It has become an essential part of modern common sense to think in this way about human thought and action. These are not to be taken at their face value as spontaneous choices but must be seen as the theoretically predictable consequences of the situations out of which they arise. And the sociological and psychological theories that have mostly been used for this purpose hitherto are vague and weak besides those that are about to come from genetics, biophysics, and biochemistry. We are at last standing on the threshold of the same sort of theoretical understanding of living things that we have had for some time of inanimate matter. When the physical basis of inheritance and the higher human activities is understood, then we shall really begin to see what makes men what they are; and this will be the main scientific business of the next century. The epoch in which the higher human activities and the specifically human freedom appropriate to them were thought of in complete isolation from physical conditions is rapidly ending. Everything human must be seen as part of the natural world in which it arises, and, like any other part, must be causally explicable. And while the older determinism could not give you chapter and verse for that belief, the newer can, in the shape of our daily increasing and detailed causal knowledge of the springs and conditions of human action.

Thus there is no doubt at all which side must win this logical war between necessity and choice. The ineluctable determination of human actions by their antecedents, which the theologians and speculative philosophers first glimpsed in abstract principle, and which Marx and Freud began to elucidate in concrete detail, is now being progressively established in field after field, with all the rigour of science. Intelligence and temperament, criminality and neurosis, originality and conformism, totalitarianism and liberalism, every aspect of human life and culture is being and will be progressively traced down to its social and biological conditions; and, as that happens, so we will think less and less in terms of choice and more and more in terms of cause. The distinctively human kind of freedom with which we began will certainly remain distinctive, but only as an exceptional intricacy of causes, not as an inexplicably spontaneous choice. We are now just at the beginning of this great intellectual revolution. We are getting into the way of regarding the criminal as diseased, not evil; the neurotic as ill, not weak; the wayward child as difficult, not naughty; and yet we still slip all too easily into the moralistic categories of vice and virtue that are the ideologist's stock-in-trade. But this compromise is unstable and will not last. Scientific analysis and technological control will soon assume the exclusive place in the management of human life that it has already taken in the management of nature. How ironical that it should have been the ideologists themselves who, by attempting to make their moralising rigorous, built up those concepts of necessitation that rule all moralising out!

8

Ideology Demolished?

WE CAN now complete the demolition of ideologies with one last small charge.

No one denies that language has strong latent powers of stimulating emotion and shaping attitudes; and no one denies that those powers can be used just as well to mould parents and citizens as to mould consumers. The ideologist's job is precisely that: to mould the moral and political attitudes of people for the benefit of some institution, old or new, conservative or revolutionary.

'Reason', 'rational', and the like are powerfully persuasive words. They tend to make us strongly favourable to anything to which they can be plausibly applied. This favourable force they get from their standard use, in which they serve to designate those processes of definition, inference, theorising, and observation by which we come to understand nature and control it for our own advantage. So great, in fact, are the advantages of the rational approach to nature, that 'reason', still more 'science', has become almost as strongly favourable a word as 'free'. Of course, this remark applies only to our particular culture. In the Germany of the thirties Hitler found it more persuasive to pour scorn on reason, and to urge his listeners to think with their blood and instincts instead of with their heads. But these are just questions of what rhetorical technique is best suited to each time and place; and the fact is that in our time and place 'reason' and 'science' carry weight, a lot more weight than 'blood' and 'instinct'.

Granted, then, that this favourable force is there to be used, what more natural than that the ideologists should seek to use it for their special purposes? If only they could plausibly represent as 'rational' or 'scientific' the considerations that they bring forward to support their party they would be much nearer to making its authority unquestioned. What is therefore wanted is some verbal ploy that will lead us to transfer our respect for reason or science to the party or the Church.

Given the mesmeric effects of repetition on the human mind, one simple step in this direction is to call the decisions of the party scientific and the declarations of the Church the words of reason, and just to go on doing so until it begins to be believed. But such crude devices can be supplemented by subtler ones. The most subtle one of all is to cast the apparatus of propaganda in the form of ratiocination. The crude reality of party interests, personal desires, and linguistic influences will then be discreetly hidden behind the masks of truth and principle and argument. This is a wonderful device. It simultaneously disguises the propagandist and lulls his unsuspecting victim. What need is there for him to be on guard against so high-minded a fellow-scientist! And this misrepresentation of influence as science is all that the elaborate talk of values and foundations really comes to.

With this observation, the demolition of ideology is in principle complete. Its logical force has been demonstrated to be nil; its persuasive force—we may hope!—has at least been weakened by having been exposed. May we not even hope that this vast monument to human credulity will soon be laid so low that it will never again be reconstructed?

The only practical arguments that a man of sense can accept are those that are addressed to his interests. If you will show me scientifically how I can get what I want and avoid what I dislike, then we can do business with each other. And no doubt many of the particular contentions of the ideologists are perfectly acceptable in this sense. Perhaps it really would be in my interest for private ownership of the means of production to be abolished, or for divorce to be forbidden. If so, show me that it is, and you will have given me perfectly good reasons for supporting those policies. What I object to are not the policies as such but the ideologies behind them, the spurious reasons that are given for policies whose connections with my interests are as difficult to establish as their connections with other people's interests are awkward to avow.

We sceptics, therefore, offer the world not an ideology

but an anti-ideology. We really do believe in reason, to which
the ideologists pay lip-service only; we believe, that is, in the
reason that proves its worth in science; we believe in empirical reason, pragmatic reason. That being so, our anti-
ideology attacks on two fronts. First it attacks the pretence
of reason, unmasking fallacy and confusion; second it
attacks the persuasive use of language, unmasking disguised
appeals to sentiment. It thus provides the ordinary man with
two invaluable weapons—of logical and of rhetorical discrimination—by which he can defend and promote his own
real interests against the power and propaganda of prevailing
institutions. In that specific sense it sets men free.

*Common sense, etc
is an ideol. position*

Third Remarks:
All Against All?

*THE sceptic has said: we men exist, as individuals, and have
our individual interests; freedom consists in getting what we
want; only those practical arguments are rational that tell
us how to get what we do want; moral and social 'principles',
and the 'beliefs' brought forward to support them, are no
more than linguistic devices by which men, individually or in
groups, try to secure their ends; the way these devices work
can be analysed, and their effectiveness can be appraised; but
over and above such technical questions of cause and effect
there is no question of an ideology being right or wrong.*

*Faced by this scepticism the ideologists would say: men
have wants indeed, but also, whether or not they know it,
objectively binding rules to live by; these rules can and must
be discovered and established by a rational investigation of
man's position in the world; that is my function; I stand by
this account of what I do even though other thinkers, who
give an identical account of themselves, claim to discover
other rules than mine and to establish them in other ways;
and I hold that scepticism in these matters is a contemptible
evasion of man's responsibility to discover the foundations
of his common life.*

*Thus the ideologists attack each other, backed by the
legions of their faithful, from the fanatics to the acquiescent.
The sceptic attacks them all; and around him stand the miscellaneous millions of the doubtful, the ignorant, the un-
concerned.*

*What are we to make of this intellectual war of all against
all? It seems to have laid waste the ordinary world of principle and purpose; how can we live in this wilderness of
doubt, or emerge from it? Of course, we must not be melo-
dramatic. We know very well that men will continue to reason and believe by instinct, no matter how little they can*

justify their doing so; and it may well be that the plain man's instinct, which intellectuals tend to castigate as carelessness and inattention, is true wisdom. But there is something repulsive—to me at least—in giving up the enquiry at this point. I feel I must prolong the search for words to convey man's reconciliation.

And perhaps this feeling is not an idiosyncrasy. Men are, by definition, biologically one; they can breed together. They have become, by recent history, scientifically, technologically, commercially, and militarily one; they must live or die together. If they are to live together in these circumstances they must become, in some form, politically one; if politically, then, in some form, ideologically. Sensing these consequences, humanity is murmuring against the sceptic, 'We must have just ideas to live by'; yet it is also murmuring, in the clash of ideologies and the shadow of the bomb, 'But those ideas, however various, must, as a matter of absolute practical necessity, yield so much to one another that, at the very least, they abjure violence.' Can these murmurs be brought together, and spoken out aloud? Who knows? The only certainty is to begin.

By way of a beginning, I suggest two steps, one moral, the other philosophical.

A rebel general at the start of the Spanish Civil War declared: 'Down with intelligence! Long live death!' That is a possible attitude—it was institutionalised by the S.S.—but our ideologists reject it, and the sceptic too; they all believe in intelligence and look forward together to some kind of human future before insisting that it should follow the pattern they prefer. But it seems to me that they all look forward too little, and insist too much. It is noticeable, for instance, that the sceptic shows an animosity to which, as a logician, he has no right, and in which he shows no prudence as a man. If he finds logical errors in ideology, well and good, let him say so; but errors are not sins, and if he attacks those who make them, let him say what he expects to gain. Will people be more likely to avoid these errors in future by being called fools, pawns, or hypocrites for having made them in the past? But, then, I must not let the animosity that the sceptic shows to others awaken animosity in me. If I attack him what shall I gain? Will he be more likely to avoid ani-

mosity in the future for being called shallow or vindictive now? I must have as much regard for him as I say that he should have for others.

Equally, the ideologists treat their rivals with hostility and the rest of mankind with ill-concealed contempt; but when they talk down to me I must not be so foolish as to copy their mistake by putting myself on a pedestal and talking down to them. If I really want to reach some understanding with them, then I must set myself to attend to what they have to say so patiently that they, perhaps, will eventually cease to preach at me, and begin to discuss with me instead. We do not sacrifice a jot of our loyalty to truth by being limitlessly patient with those with whom we disagree, in the hope that that will help to make them patient with ourselves. On the contrary: since hostile feelings tend to obscure and warp our picture of the facts before us, a policy of patience should help us to be more realistic.

It seems, then, that if we are to study ideologies and anti-ideologies profitably we must begin by adopting an attitude for designating which I suggest we use the words 'consideration' or 'regard'. By these words, therefore, I shall mean the capacity to think of the next man as your fellow, no matter what he does or says; the capacity never to give up hope of finding ways of acting and talking acceptable to both; the capacity to look at him, listen to him, and behave towards him in the manner that that hope dictates. And if that explanation seems obscure, then, on the next occasion when somebody says something that strikes you as absurd, foolish, prejudiced, offensive, or mad, instead of allowing yourself to be nettled and throwing your opinion against his, try offering suggestions as to how the difference of opinion comes about; try feeling around in the murky issues through which both of you are floundering for solid facts upon which both can stand; try listening as intently as you speak. I think that you will then become familiar with the attitude in question—with the intelligence that the rebel general wanted to abolish—and that you will find that it is its own reward.

So much for the moral step.

The philosophical step is this. It is a fact that men think; that when they think they make assumptions; that these assumptions are often contradictory; and that these contradictions are sometimes radical, in the sense that it seems im-

possible to withdraw either, or to assert both. If I maintain that X is both a mother and a Roman Catholic priest I have made contradictory assumptions (that X both is and is not a woman); but I can escape the contradiction by withdrawing whichever assumption proves, on further inspection, to be false. If I maintain both that a theory of mine is sound and that an observation is correct, and then discover that the observation is not what the theory would lead one to expect, then I am involved in contradiction, and either the observation or the theory must give way, as one or other always can. But if, on the other hand, I assert that X callously killed his wife in order to be able to marry another woman with whom he was infatuated I seem to make two assumptions, both that he could have acted otherwise, and that his action followed from a chain of causes and effects; and most people find it difficult to see how these assumptions can be either severally withdrawn or jointly asserted.

This last contradiction is one that the sceptics put bluntly before us; but it seems clear that all the issues with which we are dealing in this book involve contradictions of this radical kind. Values both must be more than tastes and prejudices, and yet cannot be; metaphysical assumptions both must be made, and yet, when made, be unintelligible by normal standards; man, as a spiritual being, is unique, and yet is just a kind of animal; freedom must be thought about, and yet the relevant facts cannot be ascertained; all men are equal, and yet, of course, are not. But in order to keep things in perspective we must note that there are many other radical contradictions of which little or nothing has been said. Such contradictions, in fact, lurk everywhere—only what, in principle, can be objectively observed can be admitted to be real; but what about my feelings? Are they not real, but unobservable objectively? Necessary truths seem to be trivially true, in virtue of the meanings of the terms that they contain; but mathematical truths, which are certainly necessary, are as certainly not trivial. It is wrong to break the law; but, surely, it is sometimes right to do so? The word 'red' means some one thing; but, amongst all the red things that there are, what is the one thing that it means? This logical phenomenon, plainly, is very general.

Now, radical contradictions are what philosophy is about. The philosopher is a man with a nose for them, and a con-

science about them. He scents them, when other men would pass them by; having done so, he brings them out into the light of day, keeps them there before us, insists that we consider them, works at them as best he can, and invites us to join his labours and accept his results. This sensitivity to radical contradiction, and this determination to resolve it, is what defines him. But then the one thing everybody knows about philosophers is that their results are discordant. There are idealists and materialists, monists and pluralists, determinists and libertarians, rationalists and empiricists. And not only do philosophers not agree in their results; they do not even agree as to how they might conceivably achieve agreement. The history of philosophy does not show a steady accumulation of universally accepted demonstrations and conclusions, as does the history of mathematics or of natural science; on the contrary, it is a strange record of new methods leading nowhere, of great reforms that leave matters much as they were, and of central problems no nearer a solution now than when they were first propounded by the Greeks.

Why on earth, you may well ask, should anyone bother himself at all with radical contradictions if so many men, of such great intelligence and integrity, have devoted their whole lives to this investigation to such small effect? But rather than consign all philosophical writings to the flames, as containing nothing but sophistry and illusion, I suggest that—for the sake of the argument at least—you add to the moral assumption of a considerate attitude the philosophical assumption that the persistence of radical contradiction— reflected in the turbulent history of philosophy—is not necessarily to be deplored. Generally speaking, of course, contradiction is deplorable. If your interest is to discover and impart the truth, or to reach some practical understanding, then to contradict yourself, and therefore to take back with one hand what you have given with the other, is self-defeating. But perhaps radical contradictions have a special part to play.

And so, since animosity towards a party to an intellectual conflict is not justified by any errors that he may commit, and tends to distort our picture of the facts, let us adopt a more constructive attitude. However firmly we stand up to those who do or say things that we find intolerable, let us not

condemn them; rather, let us open our minds to theirs
with firmness, patience, expectation. And since philosophers
have persistently failed in the attempt to put paid to radical
contradiction, let us not rush thoughtlessly into that attempt
again; rather, let us be canny, and see if we may not do
better if we aim less high.

It is possible, incidentally, that those two attitudes, the
moral and the philosophical, are related to each other. A
canny optimism? One might do worse. But, anyway, the
proof of the pudding is in the eating; so I propose to tackle
in that spirit the chaos that ideologists and anti-ideologists
have got us into, and to see what comes.

PART THREE

A PHILOSOPHER
AT WORK

9

Ideas and Power

EACH of us contains many possible men. The vindictive and the forgiving, the warm and the cold, the sensual and the abstinent, dance their complicated steps within me and take their turn to come forward to the footlights and become the man you see. In particular, we are as inclined to have contempt for one another as consideration. But we have agreed to try to make regard our normal attitude, in order to see if it increases understanding; we are to bring our considerate selves before the footlights and to keep them there, while we think them through for a time. Granted that, how far can we go with the sceptic's view that ideologies are just the instruments of power?

The trouble with his argument is that he is so obsessed with their speciousness as theories that he only considers their efficacy in terms of the hypocritical scheming of interested parties; but if we remove the blinkers of hostility— and, of course, we must have as much regard for ideologists as for anyone else—we see that the sceptic has opened up for us several striking lines of thought.

The first is that of ideological diversity. We have heard the declarations of three ideologists only, who spoke for systems very powerful in the world today; but there are many contemporary systems of which we have heard nothing, although they too are strong; and an endless array of others stretches out before us if we include the less important and the past. We have not considered the combination of racialism with protestant Christianity that inspires the rulers of the Union of South Africa, nor the new nationalisms of Africa, nor Hinduism, nor Islam, nor the pragmatic traditionalism of the British, nor Judaism, nor the Buddhism for which men and women in South-East Asia are prepared to burn themselves alive. And a comprehensive survey would have to add to these the faiths of hundreds of minor religious and political sects, the remnants of the faiths of all the separate tribal societies that are now being rolled up into the one great society of the modern world, and then the myriad ghosts, laid or still walking, of the convictions of the past.

To this diversity of doctrine there corresponds a real diversity of sentiment and conduct. Human nature being plastic, ideologies, by blessing some characteristics and damning others, help to produce a real difference in the quality of life between one people and the next. Ideologies give men a second nature. A Buddhist will burn himself alive by way of political protest, and be deemed holy for it by his co-religionaries; but a liberal will dismiss such an action as lunatic, while a traditional Christian will condemn it as a sin. To burn or not to burn : what difference could be more radical than that? And if we survey the ways in which people regard and handle sex, money, work, play, power, violence, pleasure—indeed anything in life that has ever been deemed of some importance—we meet a thousand differences, just as extraordinary, which ideologies make it their business to mark out, justify, and inculcate. It seems that there is nothing of which men are physically capable that has not been blessed or damned by some ideology or other.

In addition, ideologies are always internally complex and often inconsistent : different people can and do draw different practical conclusions from the same ideological premises. Every possible attitude towards war, from the most pacific to the most bellicose, every possible attitude towards slavery, from the most indignant to the most complacent, have been held by Christians to be dictated by their Christianity. The like is true of other religions. As for political ideologies, it is notorious how contradictory principles have been held to be self-evident (or natural) within the same society; while the present disputes between the Communist parties of Russia and of China show that the appeal to historical necessity is no more rigorous in its results for being alleged by Marxists to be scientific in its methods.

These facts of the diversity and inconsistency of ideologies certainly give the sceptic good grounds for thinking that there is something seriously wrong with the claim that ideologies make to possess exclusive truth. If, properly speaking, they are theories at all, their contradictory claims and internal inconsistencies prove that they are very bad ones; so bad—one is inclined to argue—that it is hard to see how any thoughtful and candid person can accept them.

This impression is strengthened by a look at the ways in which ideologies are propagated. Just as we are exposed, when very young, to certain particular forms of dress and table-manners, so we are exposed to a certain picture of the world; we assume the one as unthinkingly as we do the others. The fact that it is the picture of the world of those we live with means that they teach it to us by a thousand imperceptible gestures, hints, requirements, observations. Language, above all, cultivates our vision and our feelings. We learn to see just what it classifies and to feel just what it prompts, as the sceptic showed with his examples of 'thrift' and 'honour'. But this naive instruction is soon reinforced by pressures more explicit and severe. The sceptic analysed the use of metaphors and of repetition to build up an image of the world, with its attendant feelings; he might have added the effects of ritual and ceremony (the party meeting, the church service), and of solemn occasions (May Day, Christmas). He might also have considered the effects on a man's credence of having, at least, to go through the motions of professing a certain faith in order to succeed in the society that owns it, effects that are notably intensified under tyranny, where the nonconformist has to endure not ill-success nor ostracism merely, but terror. It is remarkable what a man will come to believe in order to survive. And another technique, familiar to the Inquisition, has recently been brought to a new pitch of perfection. If, over a period of weeks and months, you put a man under every kind of physical and mental pressure (hunger, pain, sleeplessness, solitude, interrogation), you can often break up the whole structure of his old beliefs and loyalties and reduce him to such a state of guilty and agonised confusion that if another ideology is offered to him as the condition of his re-acceptance by society, he will accept it so completely that, for fear of the pit from which it has rescued him, he will never let it go. We are all mildly brainwashed as children—for what happens when a child does not accept his elders' view of life?—but what was written then can sometimes be erased, and recomposed.

Now if ideologies are not only diverse and inconsistent but propagated in such ways as these, the sceptic certainly seems to have good reasons for suggesting that they are not the rational theories that they claim to be; and he reinforces that suggestion by his penetrating criticisms of their logical structure. It seems perfectly reasonable in these days to take natural science as the model of what a theory ought to be; but if we put ideologies up against the model of science we find that they fall short in all the key respects. Unlike the special terms of a scientific theory (like 'nucleus' or 'gene') the special concepts of an ideology are either (like 'God' or 'spirit') manifestly indefinable in empirical terms or else (like 'proletariat') empirically indefinable as they are used by the ideologist, who allows no observation to invalidate the statements he makes with them. Nothing can be a statement that is not ultimately falsifiable by experience; for only what is ultimately falsifiable by experience excludes some possibilities (those by which it would be falsified); and only what excludes some possibilities tells you something about the world from which they are excluded, and therefore constitutes a statement. What excludes no possibilities asserts no realities. There is thus a contradiction between logical security and empirical significance. Complete security can only be obtained by saying nothing positive; if you say something positive you must be ready to be wrong. And it must be admitted that the sceptic showed that all the ideologists he studied, faced by this dilemma, prefer security to sense. Not only so, but they make a virtue of their logical evasions. All well-developed ideologies keep amongst their armoury of intellectual weapons one in particular which enables them to deal, on their own terms, with all their rivals. Thus Marxism rules religion out from serious consideration as the sacred, and liberal democracy as the profane, camouflage of exploitation; Catholicism returns the compliment by ruling out all social faiths as the expression of inflated human pride; liberal democracy rules out both its rivals as masks of oligarchic power. On these terms, plainly, rational discussion between different ideologies cannot begin; for each doctrine is first issuing itself with a certificate of soundness, and then explaining how anybody can believe such monstrous errors as those of its opponents by means of some special theory of motivation. The opponents of the doctrine are said to embrace the errors through class interest, pride, or oligarchical pretensions, while those who maintain it claim that they do so through the pure influence of truth alone. However, it is interesting to note that having thus secured itself, on its own terms, against any possible attack, each doctrine finds it hard to keep up the appearance of disinterested truth. The sceptic is certainly right when he maintains that their writings reveal them as much more concerned to put their doctrines over than to show that they are true. The method is more rhetorical than scientific; the aim more to persuade than to convince. And the upshot of this tendency, when carried to an extreme, is sinister. If you allow yourself to think of your ideas primarily as instruments or weapons to be used on other people you inevitably cease to believe in them yourself. A weapon does not tell you how it should be used; a man who treats ideas as weapons consequently leaves himself with nothing to live by but the assertion of his own power. Not every ideologist is as candid on this point as Hitler, who used to say bluntly that the Jew of Nazi mythology had had to be invented in order that he and the Germans should have something to hate, and that the only thing the movement stood for was the power of its leader; but that is the way every ideologist is going when he allows himself to think of ideologies as forces which work profoundly on mankind and which can be used as weapons by the intelligent few who understand them. The sceptic was surely right when he said that he himself did little more than voice the scepticism to which the ideologists reduce themselves by internecine strife.

It seems, then, that no ideologist can possibly deny that ideologies exist as forces and are used as weapons; that they are diverse, changeable, somewhat arbitrary in application, and often practically inconsistent; that sociological and psychological analysis can relate them to the structure of the societies and personalities by whom they are professed; that this knowledge only elaborates the insights of the practised politician and can be used by him to manipulate people for his purposes; that the diversity, arbitrariness, and inconsistency of ideologies makes it very hard to accept their claim to be rational; and that this resistance to them can only be strengthened by the further claim that it springs from bad motives or bad faith. How can I take seriously a theory that is obliged to defend itself against my criticisms by impugning my character?

The sceptic has therefore made his case that ideologies are consequences, vehicles, and instruments of power, and has left us in grave doubt as to whether they are anything more. That doubt is the thing to be studied. But when present circumstances are taken into account there is hope as well as doubt in the connection of ideas with power. It seems to be the case that one can only think of ideas as instruments of one's own power in so far as people can, if necessary, be constrained, by the simpler kind of power called 'force', to submit to their employment. Fear, in the last resort, is the secret of persuasion; all the rhetorical and ceremonial still in the world cannot impose a faith completely upon people who are free to question it without risking their skin. But given that we are moving into an epoch in which the relations between authority and force are bound to be fundamentally changed, because the kinds of force—bombs, drugs, and the like—that are now becoming available are intolerably dangerous, may it not be the case that conditions are being created in which the relations between ideology, authority, and force will be changed too? May it not be that the intimate links of ideology with power, to which the sceptic draws attention, were due to peculiar social circumstances that are now beginning to pass away? That ideologies were combative because of the peculiar intensity of the divisions within and between societies? That their self-righteousness, exclusiveness, and hostility are temporary distortions of a rational core which it is now easier for us to discern because we must now, whatever happens, seek peace and ensure it? But the existence of such a rational core in ideological thinking must be established in the teeth of scepticism.

10

Dealing with Doubt

SUPPOSE that, shocked by the news in the morning paper, I deplore the fact that in the Union of South Africa the police can detain anyone they please indefinitely without trial. It is possible, although of course unlikely—given the fact that the people with whom we live usually share our convictions on such important matters—that my companion will question my judgment. 'What,' he may ask, 'is wrong with that?' Then, if I take his question seriously, and have the time and will to answer it, I will deploy some arguments. I may first try to state the general principle that underlies my condemnation of the South African Preventive Detention Act, and assert that arbitrary police power is always wrong. If my companion had merely been uncertain as to what it was about the situation in South Africa that I had condemned, that reply would clear the matter up; and if he shared my values it would satisfy him too. Suppose, however, it does not. 'What,' he asks, 'is wrong with arbitrary police power?' It seems that I must now bring up further values—and appropriate facts—to support the first one. I may point out, for instance, that the rule of law is the lynch-pin of all other civil and political liberties, and that arbitrary power spells as much demoralisation for those who wield it as suffering for its victims. At this point the argument is liable to get complicated, for many further facts and values are assumed in that reply. My sceptical companion may question my assumption as to the influence of arbitrary police power on other institutions, either in general or in this particular case; again, he may question my belief that this power demoralises and causes suffering, or at least that in this case it causes more suffering than it averts. Alternatively, he may concentrate his criticism more on the values that

155

I have asserted than on the facts I have assumed. He may argue that he is not convinced that so-called civil and political liberties are really good; or that the sufferings of those individuals against whom the act is used are really important; or that what I have pleased to call the demoralisation of those who execute it is really to be deplored. He will then invite me to offer more support. Taking a deep breath, I shall then try to marshal the arguments in favour of the civil and political liberties in which I believe and on which I implicitly relied in making my original comment. But whatever I say I shall obviously be relying upon further facts and values; and so soon as I have brought these assumptions to the surface my companion—apparently—can demolish them by the same simple move of saying that he does not accept them. Whatever value I rely on he has only to observe 'But what entitles you to maintain *that*?' and once again he seems to have me on the run. Unless I can think of a new move I seem to be caught in a vicious regress; and so it begins to look as if I could never have had any real reason for maintaining my original position. And that is the practical importance of the whole discussion. How can I, in the cut and thrust of life, stand up against arbitrary power, and encourage other people to do the same—as sometimes must be done, even in the most liberal country—if I can produce no solid argument to show that arbitrary power is bad? However dubious I may feel about the arguments of those who try to anchor their values in intuitive self-evidence, the authority of God, historical necessity, or whatever else, shall I not be forced to take some step of that kind? If the choice is between radical uncertainty about all my values and the acceptance of a system of belief which is external to them and by which they can be proved, must not my logical scruples about such systems be sacrificed to the imperative necessity of being sure about what I ought to do? That, anyway, is what most popular moralists contend. The trouble with modern man, they say, is that he lacks a creed, a faith to live by, a basis of absolute assurance in the shifting world; this it is that people must be given, whatever the sceptical philosopher may say. And however shocked we may be at the idea that belief may be desirable in itself, without respect to the rationality of what is believed, or to the means used to produce it, the defender of faith will not have been answered until another way of dealing with scepticism has been found.

In order to get the measure of this kind of scepticism it seems prudent to consider first of all whether it is really limited to values. Could not a similar pattern of argument be deployed against beliefs of any kind? Take the case of history. I assert that King Asoka lived in the fourth century B.C., that he was a convinced and pious Buddhist, and that he extended the empire that he had inherited. Somebody challenges these assertions, urging first that my only reason for believing them are the interpretations that are put on certain Indian manuscripts, monuments, and inscriptions—which, of course, is perfectly correct—and then that each of these interpretations could very well be false, since all our interpretations of the relics of the human past rely upon generalisations about human behaviour and a mass of previous interpretations. In order to use a given monument as evidence for the life and works of King Asoka I have to assume certain generalisations as to how objects of this kind come into existence, and then, taking for granted many other beliefs about the past—for example, the history of Buddhism and of Indian political divisions—simultaneously use those beliefs to illumine the monument, and the monument to illumine those beliefs. In fact, no argument can be made out in support of any one historical belief that does not assume a great number of other historical beliefs. It follows that doubt can always be thrown on the first belief by throwing doubt upon the rest; since beliefs about King Asoka presuppose beliefs about Buddhism in general, if the latter are uncertain so are the former too. And, in fact, the same dialectic can always be repeated. What right, it may be asked, have we got to our assumptions about the state of Buddhism in India at that time? In what way can those beliefs be supported? Only, once again, by interpreting still further evidence in the light of still further beliefs. And plainly this process is interminable. There are no historical propositions whose truth is self-evident or guaranteed from outside history. Every belief about the past assumes a multitude of others and can be questioned by raising questions about them. And so, if nothing is to be deemed rational unless it can be proved, the belief about Asoka is just as irrational as the belief in civil liberties. Universal scepticism can invade our ideas about what happened in the past just as much as it can invade our convictions as to what should happen in the future.

Nor is that the end. In order to interpret the relics of the past we have had to make use of general propositions about the powers and properties of things—for example, the proposition that stones of a certain shape could not come into existence through natural causes, but only through the agency of men, perhaps only through the agency of men who possessed a particular kind of tool. And, of course, our predictions of the future depend upon generalisations just as much as do our retrodictions of the past. Every time I pick something up or put it down, every time I look and listen, every time I eat and drink, I assume many general truths about the physical and chemical properties of what I handle, notice, or consume. I take it for granted that my pen will not explode, that the light is normal, and that this water will not poison me. We cannot act in the world or think about it without implicitly relying on the validity of some generalisations; it is largely on their rationality that the rationality of my life depends. But what supports a generalisation? Experience, it may be answered. We first observe what goes with what and then generalise our observations. But in making any single generalisation we implicitly assume a host of others. To decide whether one kind of thing—say an insect—is larger than another we must measure them—say with a ruler. In measuring things with a ruler we implicitly assume that the ruler does not change its length between one measurement and the next, an assumption resting on our general knowledge of the properties of wood or steel. All scientific instruments, of which a ruler is just the simplest, embody a great mass of generalisations about the materials of which they are made, the way they are put together, and the manner in which they are affected by other things. How then about these latter generalisations, on which we rely whenever we observe? Our assurance as to our observations rests on our assurance as to the generalisations that we use in making them: but whence does that assurance come? Plainly, by a repetition of the procedure. And so science, equally with history and valuation, is a tissue of interdependent propositions, no one of which can be established without the help of others. The sceptical argument appears therefore to be much too powerful, if it subverts anything, it subverts everything.

That this really is the case is shown when the principle of the argument is extracted from these particular cases and stated in its general form. So extracted, it is this: every proposition (in morals, history, physics, or whatever else) implies other propositions, so that its truth is inseparable from theirs; this sequence of conditions is, in the nature of the case, interminable; therefore, no belief can be secured from the risk of being upset by falsity in its unexamined conditions; therefore, everything is uncertain. Now it is plain that we generally reject this principle in practice, since we hold that propositions can be perfectly well established in history and in physics; but are we right so to reject it? If we are, what is wrong with it? And does the recognition of that central error free us from those unnerving doubts about the ground of value?

The fallacy involved in all sceptical arguments of this kind can be exposed, when the right moment comes, by a simple but penetrating question. Suppose that having condemned arbitrary police power in South Africa, and having appealed for support to the principle of the rule of law, I am being pressed hard by a hostile critic who claims to doubt the force of that principle; suppose that I have brought many facts and value up to back it; suppose that the values to which I have eventually appealed—for instance, that of the happiness of those concerned—are so fundamental that I hardly know what else I could bring forward; suppose my critic still claims to be dissatisfied, on the ground that I am still implicitly assuming further values; and suppose—as is all too likely—that he does so with an insufferable air of higher logical integrity: how am I to deal with him and his unceasing questions? Confess my inability to answer them and so let myself appear to be holding on to an indefensible position? No indeed! This is the moment to ask a question of my own. 'Tell me,' I say, 'what sort of answer would you regard as satisfactory? Under what conditions would you grant that your doubts about my condemnation had been overcome?' It is now my critic who is on the run, and I who can chase him through a series of dilemmas. For he has either to refuse to answer my question or to provide an answer to it. If he refuses to answer it, then it is he who stands convicted of irrational caprice, for it is he who is now refusing to accept a judgment, without giving any reason. So he must try to answer. But if he does so he is in precisely the same situation that I was in before; for I can now question his view as he previously questioned mine, arguing either that it does not apply to the case in hand or that it is unsatisfactory in itself. If, for example, he supports arbitrary police power by saying that it is a means to secure the rule of a particular party or race I can argue that in fact it will not do so, or else that his sectarian values, even supposing that there is anything to be said for them at all, are insignificant by comparison with the evils that follow from trying to secure them in this way. He is now faced by the final dilemma. Since he, no more than I, can decline to support his values by further argument, on pain of standing convicted of irrational caprice, either he must continue to argue with me, as I with him, bringing more values and facts to bear in the hope of discovering at last a common platform on which agreement between us can be built, or he must have recourse to arguments of a different kind and claim, perhaps, that his value is self-evident, or the revealed command of God, or the present outcome of historical necessity. But he has already proved that such metaphysical arguments are worthless, being merely the concealed assertion of the individual's arbitrary will. One man's intuitions, one man's God, one man's historical necessity, is found in hard fact to conflict flatly with another's; argument between them has been made impossible by the sheer metaphysical exclusiveness professed by each; and all that is left is will and power.

This result is remarkable. The sceptic who was criticising me for my irrationality has been forced to abandon that criticism and take part in a discussion—presumably, therefore, a rational discussion—with me. At least, if he does not do so, he must either remain in a state of doubt which he can neither explain nor justify, or else take refuge in some metaphysical dogma. Thus radical doubt and solid dogma, which seem at first sight to be poles apart, prove on inspection to have something in common: in both, co-operative discussion has been abandoned; in both, caprice has been embraced. But what precisely does that mean? How does it come about? And what is the nature of this co-operative discussion that is the alternative to doubt and dogma?

The simple but penetrating question that put the sceptic on the run was this: under what conditions would you, the sceptic, grant that your doubts about my condemnation of arbitrary police power had been overcome? That question forced him either to join in the discussion—and so implicitly to admit its rationality—or to be convicted in his turn of some kind of arbitrariness. But what gives the question that special force? What crucial weakness of the sceptic's argument does it touch? His argument really fell into two parts. The first part pointed out that all our assertions in morals, history, physics, or any other field of thought, are connected with endless other assertions by whose truth they therefore stand or fall; the second part concluded that because those others are really endless, and so cannot be checked, all our assertions are, in a crucial sense, irrational and insecure. The first of these two points must be admitted. Our thinking really is systematic in the sense defined; its parts depend on one another for their sense and strength in ways that can never be exhaustively examined, since every assertion makes assumptions that need to be examined in their turn. But the sceptic's conclusion does not follow from this conceded premise; it does not follow that because the work of reason is endless, every one of its supposed achievements must be insecure. And what our simple, penetrating question does is to reveal the fallacy of that alleged conclusion. To go back to the concrete case: if I have condemned some action of the police, and supported my condemnation by appealing to the value of the rule of law, it is no criticism of my position merely to point out that the validity of the principle of the rule of law itself depends on further assumptions, and shares such weaknesses as they may have. The critic must show, or at least try to show, that those assumptions really are weak; and to do that he must make assumptions of his own. No doubt is thrown on a contention by saying that things might be otherwise; some positive reason must be given for supposing that they are.

The principles of this argument can now be set out formally. Suppose that I do any such thing as make a prediction that the weather will be fine, pass a judgment that someone else's act was wrong, buy an unusually expensive object, or hit someone in the face: I may be asked to justify what I have said or done. Of course, I need not be. My action may pass unnoticed. Alternatively it may seem to those who notice it too indifferent, or too obviously right, or too obviously wrong, to raise the question of support. However, they may be attentive and dubious enough to question me. Indeed I may, without prompting, be dubious enough to question myself. A matter of justification has then arisen, or appears to have arisen. But we have seen that this appearance can be deceptive; doubt can seem to have been thrown on something when really it has not. The truth is that before a demand for justification need be taken seriously by those of whom it is made, various conditions must be met by those who make it; if these conditions are not met the demand lacks force, and can properly be brushed aside. What, then, are they? Four, in fact. The questioner must be prepared, first, to say exactly what the thing is that should be justified; second, to explain why justification seems to be required; third, to specify the conditions under which he would agree that justification had been given; and, fourth, to give plausible reasons for imposing those particular conditions. The character of the view or action and of its alleged fault, the standards it should satisfy and the rationality of those standards: those four points must be cleared up by the questioner if his intervention is not to be fairly dismissed as irrelevant or silly.

That the view or action in question should be clearly specified may seem a point too obvious to be worth a mention, but that is not so. Suppose that I have said 'It will be fine this afternoon', and am seriously asked why, my first move may well be to explain that I had not so much asserted it as just expressed a vague expectation. After all, the form of words, 'It will be fine this afternoon', may convey a guess just as well as an assertion, and the manner of the utterance —its serious tone, its firm pronouncement—usually fixes which of these it is supposed to be. But I may have spoken carelessly, or a noise may have drowned my intonation, although not my words, so that my companion has mistaken their intent. And this possibility is of great importance. The issues that arise about an assertion are quite different from those that arise about a guess: evidence can be demanded for assertions, while the utmost that can be asked of guesses is that they should not be wild. Likewise, supposing I am asked to justify my having struck another person I may deny that 'struck' is a correct description, saying that he had seemed to fall and that I had put out my hand to hold him. A question of justification could just as well arise, of course, about this action. I may have tried to help him tardily, or without making a real effort. But these questions are of quite a different kind from those that would arise if it is assumed that the action in question was a blow. Thus, difficulties can crop up about the nature of the thing to be justified, and when they do they must be dealt with.

From the thing we move to its supposed fault. When there is no doubt about the thing there may well be doubt about what is alleged to be wrong with it. If I have plainly asserted that it will rain but have not been near the window, or talked to anyone about the matter, or listened to a forecast, the demand for justification is natural: I have had no access to the kind of data that is needed to support the statement. The demand for justification is also natural if, while I have had access to the facts, I have put an odd interpretation on them, saying that it will rain in spite of clear skies and a favourable forecast. In either case there is an apparent fault; rightly or wrongly, I have departed from the standard pattern of procedure, and it is such departures, normally, that must be justified. But where there has been no such departure, no question of justification arises—unless, which is the next question, the standard pattern of procedure is itself in question. If I have done all the proper things (predicting the weather in accordance with the forecast and the look of the sky, helping someone who has fallen and cried out) a demand for justification is just silly, and can be neglected, unless those who make it are prepared to explain why, on this occasion, the proper thing was not good enough.

This is the next issue. I may disagree with my questioner, holding that what he alleges as a fault was nothing of the kind; the very same behaviour he may condemn as rude I may admire as independent. Alternatively, while admitting it to be a fault in one respect I may hold that this was outweighed by other merits. A broken promise may save a life; a mistake may be both harmless and instructive. In this I am objecting to my questioner's standards, either in themselves or with respect to the relative importance that he attaches to them; and, if I make a case against his standards, it is up to him to show that they are sound. To put it differently: if, having listened to my defence, he continues to demand from me a justification of what I have done, he must be prepared to say under what conditions he would agree that the action had been justified, and to show that those conditions are reasonable. To throw doubt upon an action or opinion it is not enough merely to express doubts about it; one must give the grounds for the doubt, and reasons for those grounds. It is not enough for the sceptic to point out that all statements make endless assumptions and that some of these assumptions may be wrong; if his doubt is not to be swept aside as silly he must give reasons for supposing that in fact they are. But in giving reasons he must make assumptions of his own. If he is to enter the debate at all he must lay himself open to criticism in just the same way as those have done who entered it before him. And that means that if, of set purpose, he is not going to accept *any* of the general standards, the values, in terms of which, together with relevant facts, other people justify their practical positions, he must be prepared to say what would, in his eyes, constitute a justification, and give good reasons for holding that this standard of his own is the one to accept.

Now what the sceptic said, by way of anticipating this demand, was that, for him and for any other sensible person, only those practical arguments are rational and cogent which show that what they recommend is in the interest of the individual to whom they are addressed. To be given a good reason for doing or accepting something I must be shown that it is, directly or indirectly, what I want. Beyond my desires there is nothing to which anybody can appeal. I want what I want. If something else can be shown to be essential to my wants, well and good; I want that too, and a solid reason has been given why I should pursue it. If not, what is it to me? Of course, amongst the things that I shall want, if I happen to be a benevolent person, will be the happiness of some other people; to that extent, what they want is what I want too. I shall then be in favour of whatwhatever makes for the satisfaction of their desires, and I shall have been given a good reason for a policy if it has been shown to do so. Equally, if other people's discontent affects me adversely, either by being disagreeable to behold or by leading them to act in ways that cause me trouble, then I shall have been given a good reason for a policy when it has been shown to lessen their discontent, and so my inconvenience. But however much I must take other people's interest into account in order to promote my own, it is only my own that matters when it is a question of deciding what to do. Here, and here only, do we reach the bedrock of common sense. Ideals, duties, rules, principles, values: all such talk is mystification. The only thing that is real and solid is what I want; the only practical arguments that make sense are those that show me how to get it.

Are we to accept this view?

Within certain limits it is plain that we must do so. Nobody doubts that one kind of good practical argument is that which shows what is and what is not conducive to our interests. If you are salting your food and I suggest that you stop, as it is pretty salty already, I have given you a good reason for desisting, but one which directly concerns your own interests, and nothing more. Who else is affected, if you spoil your dish, but you? We use this form of argument, very properly, a hundred times a day: when we scratch a place that tickles, drink a glass of water, or put on a jersey as the day turns cold. But is it the case that practical arguments are only cogent if they can be reduced to one that has this form?

Assuming the normal conditions of a comfortable society those examples have an important character in common: no one else, in such circumstances, is seriously affected by how much salt I eat or water I drink, by whether I give myself a scratch or don a jersey. But suppose that I have several dependants and that for my heart's sake I should eat no salt at all, or that the water-supply has broken down and that this is the last glassful in the house, or that I am taking part in a ceremony when scratching would offend, or that my friend, being ill, feels the cold and needs the jersey more than I do: suppose, in fact, that I am in a situation where my wants clash with other people's: does the sceptic's principle still work? Is it enough to say, when wants conflict, that all I can rationally take into account are my own interests, even granted that they benevolently or prudently include my interest in my neighbour's satisfactions? And that question means: are there any situations in which we find ourselves that cannot be thought out purely on those terms?

Suppose that you and I find ourselves caught in a conflict of desires; each wants his own way and both cannot get it, be the matter anything from which of us shall drink a glass of water to which of us shall control the means of production. One possibility is that we shall fight until one or both of us are destroyed; another that, with or without fighting, one of us will decide that the game is not worth the candle, it being more in his interest to give way, or at least to give way up to a point the other finds acceptable in *his* own interests, than to prolong the struggle. Given that we are both intelligent people, who realise that complete victory is either impossible or involves sacrifices out of proportion to its gains, and given that each realises that the other realises this, we shall try to enter on negotiations and find a formula. This formula must be a reconciling formula; that is, it must offer us a pattern of life (large or small, enduring or momentary) in which we both feel, given the facts of our desires, that we can live more satisfactorily (or less unsatisfactorily) than on any other obtainable terms. But plainly such a formula is useless except in so far as each of us sticks to it and has a reasonable expectation of the other sticking to it too, even if, from moment to moment, it goes against the grain to do so. It is in the longer-run interests of both that the formula should stand above the shorter-run interests of either; that is, that the formula should be held by each to bind both. We have here the pure logical origin, as opposed to the complex historical forms, of the concept of value. Given two or more people—animals, that is, who can establish facts, feel satisfactions, and form policies—and given that those policies interact, as must indeed happen, with varying effects on their respective satisfactions, they cannot but evolve the concept of a binding formula for common action. The formula may be particular (what to do about this glass of water) or general (what to do about sexuality or violence); it may, that is, be a common decision or a common value; but I simply cannot run my life as a thinking animal, interacting as it does with the lives of other thinking animals, except within a framework of formulae which stand above any one of us because they are acceptable (at least up to a point, and for the time being) to us all. We thinking animals cannot have interests of our own without also having values that are common; I cannot therefore stop thinking in terms of values and merely think in terms of my own interests. It follows that the sceptic is not entitled to say that arguments about values are vain if the only reason he can give for that contention is that valid practical arguments must appeal to interests alone. And so unless the sceptic can produce some other reason for not taking part in the discussion of disputed values, on the basis of other values, assumed for the time being, then he really must take part in it, on pain of debarring himself by his irrelevance from saying anything at all.

Do you find the step just taken, from interests to values, clear and unavoidable? If not, imagine yourself trying to pursue your own interests with a systematic and rigorous exclusion of any thought about the interests of others and the devising of common formulae for your interacting lives. Would you, in those circumstances, have any idea as to what your interests were? To carry out that intellectual experiment you must of course imagine yourself so powerful that you need pay no attention, by way of prudence, to what other people want; for we have seen that prudence, vis-à-vis other thinking animals, carries obligation with it. Well, then, imagine that you are so powerful that you need consider no one in seeking what you want: do you find that you want anything? Or do you only want to shatter everything to bits, since, without the bitter-sweet discipline of common purpose, no heart's desire remains to which you would remould it? There are moments of frustration when we feel like that; moments when, having tried all forms of co-operation with those near us, and failed to find one that works, we only hanker to destroy. And perhaps it is only if we make periodic visits to this pit, where interests and values are both swallowed up in limitless destruction, that we find out what interests and values are and how they depend on each other; perhaps it is the Hitlers of this world, the universal wolves, who are its strongest moral teachers.

So we have got the sceptic on the move; he must either enter the discussion of values, within the world of other values, or else exclude himself by triviality; but does that help us with our own problem? Can I be any surer now of the ground I stand on when I condemn police methods in South Africa? By condemning those methods I make a claim for freedom—for freedom, in this case, from arbitrary police power. I concede that if my claim is not itself to be arbitrary it must be given support. I also concede, following the sceptic's earlier arguments, that that support must consist of further facts and further values, from which it can be shown to follow. Since further values have been used to support it, still further values must, if required, be brought forward in support of them. I support one value by an endless regress into others. But all that this argument against the sceptic has achieved, it may be said, is to involve him in the same regression. It has been shown that he cannot cast doubt on a moral position merely by observing that it makes assumptions; he must make a case against those assumptions, in doing which he is bound to make assumptions of his own, which I can criticise as well as he can mine. But how does criticising him help me to find a ground for my belief in civil liberties? What do I gain by getting someone else into my own predicament?

The answer is that I gain everything. Hitherto, in all these critical investigations of our thought about values in general, and the values of freedom in particular, it has been implicitly assumed that if our thought is to be rational, all the logical ills that have been noted must be completely cured. The implication has been one of all or nothing. The sceptic implicitly assumed that thought about values could only go forward as respectable and rational if the influence of feelings could be excluded, the regression from one value to another ended, the facts of the case made clear, the originating power of human will established, and the disturbing influence of metaphysics annulled; and, since it appeared that none of these reforms was possible, the upshot of the whole attempt to clarify our practical thinking was to make it even more obscure. But why should we assume that those defects are fatal, so long as any trace of them remains? Why should it be taken for granted, which is the present theme, that for our thought about values to be rational it must in no sense be regressive? Obviously because it is assumed that no thinking can be rational that does not finally demonstrate the truth of its conclusions. But why should we assume that? May it not be the manner of our thinking that makes it rational, rather than the finality of its results? That, certainly, was what began to transpire when I pressed the sceptic on the problem of regression. I did not prove, I did not begin to prove, that my condemnation of arbitrary power was right; I merely got him to enter the discussion as to whether it was or not. The moment he stops merely saying that my position is dubious, the moment he begins to give positive reasons for holding that it may or should be doubted, the moment that he abandons the mere appeal to his own interests, the moment he therefore offers value assumptions of his own as a basis for discussion: from then on he and I are involved as equals in a common enterprise, and it is in the process of that common enterprise that we find the only basis that our thought about anything requires and can receive. In matters of reason it is not just that to travel hopefully is better than to arrive: it is that there is no final destination, and that to travel hopefully, co-operatively, and systematically is, in itself, the goal. Thus the sceptic and the dogmatist do share an illusion. The sceptic says that doubt is endless and irremediable. The dogmatist says that it can be ended, but only by adopting his definitive solution. Both say or imply that vagueness, incompleteness, and disagreement are all completely bad. Both yearn for an intellectual world in which all those bad things have been abolished, and so the minds of all men made certain, clear, and in accord. Neither will accept the life of reason as it is, in which doubt and vagueness, incompleteness and disagreement, are just as much the inspiration of our thinking as they are its flaws; in which the highest satisfaction is to overcome them in one place in order to face them in another; and in which each of us finds his own security, not in a final system of conclusions to which others must accede, but in an endless process of investigation in which all can join.

If only we could seize the concept of reason that is struggling to the surface here, set it up, make it good, and take our stand upon it, then the problems of freedom might become much more intelligible, and easier to handle. We live in a world in which change is swift and comprehensive, force no longer feasible as a means of change, and negotiation therefore crucial. Negotiation is always about freedom: what is at stake is always *which* powers of action of *which* men and women should go forward and *which* held back. But current in the world are dogmas about freedom: grand systems of ideas that claim to demonstrate that only the release of certain particular powers deserves the name of freedom, and that all counter-claims are not only false, but deluded or perverse. Equally current in the world is the

sceptical reaction to such dogma, which dismisses all serious
thinking about freedom as devoid of any rational basis. Both
doubt and dogma strangle negotiations: both deny the possibility of a common quest for common principles in the
face of disagreement and confusion, the doubter saying that
there can be no such quest, the dogmatist that there can be,
but that the principles to which it leads must be his own.
But supposing we could see, as the heart of reason, the endless common quest for common principles through all uncertainty, disagreement, and confusion, and supposing we
could come to feel that it is good just as much for what it is
as for what it does, then all our thought and negotiation
about freedom would take on a different air. If reason is
seen rather as a co-operative enquiry than as a vision of
truth, it may not be so hard to understand how it fits in with
the play of feelings and with the infinite network of causes
and effects of which our feelings form a little part. If we
learned to see the investigation of human facts and the
establishment of human values as part of the immense
adventure of changing the world, and changing himself with
it, upon which modern man is irresistibly engaged, we might
well find the obscurity of the facts and the uncertainty of
the values less repellent and more manageable. Even the
metaphysical positions of the materialist or the theologian
might begin to assume a more constructive form. We men,
to avoid and to control the use of force, are debating and
negotiating freedom. For the debate to be rational and constructive we must always seek to know for which human
powers freedom is being claimed, and why. But we cannot
reasonably demand immediate and clear answers to those
questions; for human powers change, as men act on the
world and on themselves. Men's powers of action are not
set; they are created out of each other in an endless sequence;
and if one part of the work of self-creation lies in practical
work, another lies in pondering, imaginatively and search-
ingly, our rising powers. Man must feel out for what he
might be while he takes note of what he is. When therefore,
standing upon reason as activity, we have excluded metaphysical systems in their forms as dogma, we may yet perhaps be able to accept them as explorations, perhaps essential
explorations, of the powers of man.

II

Schemes and Images

WHILE we think about freedom our hearts beat, our digestions proceed, and we grow a bit older. These activities of our organism are essential to it; but they proceed entirely, or almost entirely, outside our consciousness. We are not aware of them, and do nothing about them. Yogis do indeed claim to be able to perceive and control them, but this claim, though curious, cannot amount to very much. We may extend consciousness a little beyond its usual limits, but the fine physiological structure of our lives remains outside the range of the subtlest introspection and intensest will. Simply by taking thought we can no more control our metabolism or senescence than we can add one cubit to our stature.

Breathing is often as unconscious, but it is never far below the surface of attention. Consciousness rocks upon it like a boat on waves; and when we are learning to sing, or trying to relax, or struggling to master our temper or our fear, the deliberate control of its movement becomes for a while our main concern. This difference between heart and chest—which corresponds, of course, to differences between those parts of the nervous system that control them—is marked in language by the fact that we say 'we breathe' but only 'our hearts beat'. Respiration is something that we do (those idioms suggest), while palpitation simply happens.

The number of activities of both these different kinds is large, and the relations between them are complicated. Other notable activities of the first kind are those by which our organisms adjust themselves to changes of temperature and humidity around them, and those by which they mobilise their resources in the face of danger or on the invasion of microbes; amongst the second one can count fidgeting, posturing, gesturing, walking, talking, and the like. None of these last, of course, is essential to our lives, as respiration is; but, still, we must move in one way or another; and while we are often only half conscious, if that, of the performance, we can become fully conscious of it at any moment, and then can exercise strict control over what, in this sense of the word, we do.

When looking for good examples of human activity that take place outside consciousness it is natural to take those basic physiological functions which, like digestion, are common to man and other animals. But even those activities which are most distinctively human proceed to a great extent outside the scope of conscious awareness and control. As the speaker begins his speech, as the lover stretches out his hand, as the artist lets his pencil move across the paper, each normally has a rough idea of what he is going to do, and why and how he is going to do it. But the idea is for the most part very rough; its origin and outcome are obscure; the mainsprings of even our most important and significant actions are hidden from us; their detailed execution takes place only under the crudest supervision of the deliberate mind. And this is just as true of our simplest actions. I pick up my pen: what could be simpler, what more plainly under my control, than that? But what precisely do I know of how and why I do it? Almost nothing. For some reason or other I set myself to do it, and then I find that, somehow or other, it gets done. Thus, in the smallest as in the largest things, in those actions which we call conscious hardly less than in those which, like disease resistance, do not enter consciousness at all, or which, like digestion, only do so in the vaguest form, the field of conscious attention and effort is surrounded by a vast unknown.

It is natural to think first of the physiological unknown, for every obscure ache and pain reminds us of it, but we must not restrict ourselves to that dimension. Marx began to show how the broad social structure in which the individual lives determines, unbeknownst to him, the pattern of his thought and the colour of his feeling; Freud did the same for the finer structure of the family; and they were only skimming the surface of the matter. We can be as certain, in general, that genetic processes are decisively determining the human future as we are ignorant, in particular, of how they are doing so; and who knows what hidden consequences will follow from the elimination of toil and poverty from man's life by means of industrialisation? In our social, as in our personal, lives, that mixture of perception, understanding, policy, and will that we call 'reason' plays a small part only; enveloped and penetrated by infinite forces of which, in spite of all our science, it only has the faintest inkling, its powers of action are fitful, miscellaneous, and short-term.

To recognise that the theoretical sensitivity and the practical power of reason are very limited is, in matters of ideology, the first step to wisdom; the sceptic was right to insist that ideologists propound solutions for human problems on a scale and with a confidence out of all proportion to the realities of our knowledge of fact, or to our power to co-ordinate our actions in the light of it. The second step to wisdom is to recognise that reason, such as it is, arises out of more primitive forms of communication and remains immersed within them. To reflect on the processes of falling in love, or of understanding the mood of an old friend, or of realising that a stranger has a mean or generous disposition, is to become aware that we have many modes of communication anterior to language, and that these play a main part in our most subtle and human relationships. In such cases, speaking only puts a public seal on a private treaty. The art of rhetoric—to a few aspects of which the sceptic drew attention—is to enrich the overt messages of language with a hundred such tacit messages of tone and bearing, which prepare the way for what is said, and shadow out its implications.

The rules of language are immensely complicated. If one considers the great range of uses to which we put the one word 'to', one readily understands why the attempt to automatise translation from one language to another is proving so difficult. This constellation of uses is so involved that reducing it to simple rules, uniformly correlated with those of another natural language, is an extremely complicated problem. Indeed, while we can be fairly sure that this problem will in the end be solved for the routine, descriptive use of language, it seems inconceivable that we shall ever be able to automatise the translation of poetry, where communication relies upon the subtlest powers of words. That being so, it is remarkable that small children can master this complicated instrument as quickly and easily as they do. How can they learn, intuitively and without apparent effort, all those complexities of a word like 'to', whose analysis still defeats logicians? And the same is true of words which, like 'good' and 'bad', are central to the analysis of ideology: when one thinks of the great range of circumstances in which those words are used, it is puzzling how children learn so soon to use them correctly. But this fact becomes less puzzling when we put the learning process back into its human context. Long before the infant starts to speak it is elaborately—if intuitively—trained by its mother in co-operative enterprises. The learning of 'good' and 'bad' only formalises the common sense of achievement and frustration, of the permitted and the forbidden, of peace and hostility, which each child's elders establish between it and themselves by thousands of daily examples, gestures, caresses, punishments, smiles, rewards, rebukes, hints, and endeavours. Our knowledge of good and evil began in the cradle long before we learned the words. But that does not make the learning of the words, and the development of their meaning in the growing mind, any the less important. On the contrary, it is absolutely crucial. So long as we learn approval and disapproval in an intuitive way, as approval of this thing and disapproval of that one, we do indeed acquire particular patterns of acceptance and rejection, but we have no means of asking ourselves whether those patterns themselves, really and truly, should be accepted or rejected; we are shackled intellectually to the habits that we have acquired. And 'good' and 'bad' themselves will carry at first this conservative suggestion, being taken as convenient short names for the established mode of life. But they are names with a difference: they have a demon in them. Even under an established mode of life they are applied to a great diversity of things, between which there is no discernible similarity beyond the fact that they actually are approved or disapproved by the people in question. And so the demon stirs into life. If the approved things have nothing in common but the fact of their approval, why should not other things be approved instead? And a quick look at the world, inspired by that suggestion, shows that in fact they are. But if other things can be approved instead, why should I approve of these? By 'good' we can approve of anything; but if we have a word like 'good', by which we can approve of anything, we must also have a word like 'bad', by which we can disapprove of them instead; and so there has entered into life the capacity to look at every habit, situation, or belief, no matter how natural it may seem, and wonder whether it might not be better than it is, or whether it may not, after all, be simply bad. Forthwith, the whole array of words in which our accepted values are embodied, from the relatively abstract, like 'free', to the relatively concrete like 'generous', are cast off from their factual moorings; forthwith, everything that we encounter, feel, think, try, or say, hovers at ceaseless risk between what should be or should not; forthwith, we have to learn to live, come what come may, with this two-faced invader of our animal calm.

One supreme theoretical question of the next half-century is: how precisely do beings with this 'knowledge of good and evil' emerge, when matter gets organised in increasingly complicated forms? How do choice, self-criticism, invention, and all the other qualities that we regard as specifically human take their definite place within the order of nature? Many human activities of calculation and control, and even the more elementary forms of judgment, can already be carried out by computers; soon we may succeed in simulating the whole behaviour of simple organisms; soon we may be able to show how, in principle at least, when machines achieve a degree of complexity much higher than the present, their behaviour begins to take on forms which, though they may yet be much simpler, are yet qualitatively of the same type as those which the child's behaviour takes on as it learns to plan and choose. There seems to be no reason why computers should not reach a level of inventiveness so near our own that we would begin to regard them with respect; while the fact that we beget children, but only build machines, would begin to lose the significance that it has now. Then men will indeed appear as 'unusually intelligent and sensitive animals' and no more. But meanwhile, in confident anticipation of these discoveries, we must just take the existence of the higher critical capacities as a fact; suspending judgment on their biological basis, we must follow out their intellectual implications.

The sceptic put his finger on the decisive implication when he showed that the goodness or badness of a thing can never be established by appealing simply to the kind of thing it is, and nothing more. If we take care to describe the kind of thing it is in terms that are absolutely value neutral, as we always can, then it is always logically possible to view it as either good, bad, or indifferent, however morally obvious one such view may seem to us to be, and however morally repulsive or absurd the others. We may, for example, be offered, as a 'necessary value truth', the judgment that cruelty is wrong. But 'cruelty' is plainly a pejorative term; and that pejorative element must be removed if the judge is to be more than a platitude that repeats with 'wrong' the condemnation already pronounced by means of 'cruelty'. Shall we then say that what is wrong is the infliction of pain for the sake of the pleasure that doing so gives to the inflictor? At first sight one certainly gets the impression that the phrase 'infliction of pain for the sake of pleasure' is purely descriptive, containing no tacit value judgment, while yet the conduct it describes both is and must be wrong. But the deceptiveness of this appearance is revealed by considering what would happen if most people began to find the pleasure that some now do in certain pains—say, the moderate cut of a whip. Suppose people really did generally come to acquire this taste, as they do often come to acquire the taste for bitter drinks that children find repulsive: would there be anything more wrong in giving a friend a cut than in standing him a whisky and soda? The fact of the matter is that pains are so generally disliked that the word 'pain' normally implies repulsion. But if we remove this implication by some suitable periphrasis the original value judgment begins to lose its appearance of necessity, although we may continue to maintain it on other grounds. Doing things to people that give them sharp sensations may be right or may be wrong, depending on the circumstances; and taking pleasure in doing them is or is not permissible accordingly. But now it will be said: let us, then, in the light of these considerations, restate in full what was really meant by the original judgment, and say that what is always and necessarily wrong is the infliction of sharp sensations for the sake of pleasure, when the sensations are disliked by the person on whom they are inflicted, and can therefore properly be called pains, in the pejorative sense. Have we here reached a necessary value? A valuation that follows logically from the facts, as stated? I do not think so. It would be perfectly possible, after all, for the person on whom the sensations were inflicted to dislike them indeed, and so to call them 'pains', in so far as that term implies repulsion, while yet thinking that this dislike was weak or foolish, and therefore that it was perfectly proper for another person to inflict the pains and even to take pleasure in the process. It is in this spirit, for example, that we say of someone who has defeated us that we do not grudge him his satisfaction, provided that we think that his victory was justified, or anyway was fairly gained. In other words, even the infliction of unwelcome pain can be innocent in the context of certain special values, although this situation is relatively so rare that 'pain' normally implies as much disapprobation as dislike. But once we remove the question-begging valuations that use and wont write into language—even into such plain words as 'pain'—infinite avenues of choice open out all around us; and once we begin to look at the facts of history and anthropology from this height of philosophical abstraction, we perceive that down every single avenue of choice, however mad or monstrous it looks to us as we go down our own, some other company of men has made its way. Everything that men can do has been held by someone to be good, or bad, or indifferent.

The peculiar significance of the words 'good' and 'bad' for life is that they, more than any others, have become the linguistic vehicles by which this infinite capacity for choice plays upon our ways of living, tightening one, loosening another, and keeping all of them alive. By having been gradually purged of descriptive meaning until they are no longer tied in any way to any feature of the world, 'good' and 'bad' enable us to contemplate as possibilities an infinite variety of values, an infinite array of schemes of life. And although the capacity divides us in that way, it unites us in another; for I share the power of judgment even with those who use it in ways most alien to mine. My good may be your bad, my bad your good; but 'good' and 'bad' are ours.

The clue to the arguments of all the ideologists is that they misconstrued this situation. They are not prepared to recognise the interminable openness of the value judgment. They contend that 'good' and 'bad' can be attached so rigorously—by means of faith, utility, self-evidence, or historical necessity—to the particular ways of life they favour that it is irrational to favour any other. But against this the sceptic proved conclusively that these alleged attachments of our power of choice to given ways of life are not rigorous at all, but mere equivocations. The alleged demonstrations of morality from grounds outside itself just do not work. Subsequently, he tried to show that no attachment—no value claiming to lay down what is good for people rather than what just suits me—can be rational at all. But I dislodged him from this radical doubt about all values by showing that when I take the question of what suits me completely out of the context of what suits people, nothing suits me any more; since I can only get what I want with the co-operation of others who choose too, what suits me must eventually cohere with what suits them; if the discipline of this co-operation is removed, desire degenerates into frenzy or indifference. Therefore the sceptic cannot set up the principle of 'what suits me' as the only principle in terms of which a course of action can be rationally commended to me; therefore—on pain of excluding himself from the discussion altogether—he must talk in terms of values. He must advance ideals and rules for action and, when challenged, support those with others; he must reject an exclusive appeal to self-interest for being just as vacuous as the various appeals of ideologists to faith or history or whatever else. In fact, he must remember who he is. He sits there reasoning, but he is not a just reasoner. He can abstract from his own circumstances for the sake of argument; but they do not cease to be his circumstances because he has abstracted from them; and his conclusions will be false if they conflict with the circumstances from which he has abstracted. As a man he must co-operate with others, no less capable of thought and choice than he is; the little word 'we', which he happily uses of himself and them, in their capacity as reasoners, he must also use of himself and them in their capacity as men of action.

It is therefore necessary that I should have some values—some principles that I feel we should obey, and some ideals that I feel we should pursue. But it is one thing to say that it is necessary to have some values or other, and another to say that some particular values are necessary. I can combine an unqualified respect for principles as such with only qualified respect for the claim of any given principle to be binding. And not only can I do so, but I must. When I consider how tricky it is to apply my values to concrete cases; how often values conflict with one another in the event; how constantly I must deal with moral relations which demand co-operation between myself and others, while no existing value shows the way: then I am forced to admit that necessary as values are in general, none is necessary in particular.

Novelty, the third of those three aspects, is the most important. In fact the first two, application and conflict, are parts of it. I am faced by a problem in the application of my values when my routine methods do not seem to fit the special case in hand—as when I do not know just how to tell an awkward truth to an unstable person; I am faced by a problem of conflict when unusual circumstances bring into collision two values which normally run parallel—as when telling the truth would endanger someone's life. It is the unusualness of the situation which, in either case, shows up the inadequacy of my scheme of values. And this sort of novelty inevitably crops up even if the basic conditions of life remain unchanged. Chance is always contriving situations for which existing values are inadequate: that is what fiction and drama are about. Men have to find ways of dealing co-operatively with such unusual situations: that, largely, is what ideology is about. We may be as sceptical as we please, but still we have to think and act together in those frequent cases when accepted values do not tell us how. 'Ideology', as used here, refers not only to a set of values but also to a view of human nature in which they are embedded; and if the sceptic proved that the values are never embedded in the view in such a way that they are demonstrable by its means, he was wrong in concluding that the view must be hypocritical nonsense. It has another role instead.

The nature of this role stands out impressively from the use that the American Presidents make of the concept of equality. 'Equal', like 'free', is a positive value word; outside mathematics and measurement its normal function is to express a favourable attitude, as is shown by the fact that people who are opposed to situations that are commended by others for their equality tend to have recourse to such obviously hostile phrases as 'soulless uniformity' or 'drab monotony'. But 'equal', again like 'free', is neither quite abstract, like 'good', having no constant descriptive meaning at all; nor quite concrete, like 'brave', having a descriptive meaning which confines its use to a narrow segment of human conduct. It has a descriptive meaning, which restricts its range of use; but that meaning is so indefinite that it has to be supplemented by the context on each particular occasion. To believe in equality is to believe, roughly, that people ought to be treated alike, especially by the state, in certain respects in which they are, or tend to be, treated differently; but which those respects are is not laid down by the meaning of the word. People can therefore use the word, with equal linguistic right, to commend or condemn one and the same state of affairs. A conservative Catholic could commend for its equality a social situation in which all enjoy the same access to the ministrations of his church, while a liberal or a socialist could condemn it because the rich have a stronger position than the poor in the courts or in the control of the economy. Therefore, when somebody commends a situation for its equality we have always to establish, if the context leaves it at all uncertain, precisely what he is supporting.

He may, of course, be supporting several different things. When the American revolutionaries proclaimed the equality of man they were entering the lists for civil and political liberties. There should be no taxation without representation, no laws giving privileges to religious groups, no trials in which influence could prevail over justice, no customs requiring special deference to rank. This list was extended by some and restricted by others; notably—and throughout American history—it has been boldly extended by some to include a measure of restraint upon great concentrations of economic power, and carefully restricted by others from any such 'subversive' implication. Surveying the debate on this point, and others like it, the sceptic would certainly conclude that the idea of equality is moonshine, and the use of the word mere hypocritical misrepresentation of the interests of groups. This view has in fact been taken, by some historians, of the use of the term by both Lincoln and his opponents in the struggle between the northern and southern states over the abolition of slavery. When Lincoln spoke out for the equality of the individual, irrespective of national or racial origin, and when his opponents resisted—as they are still resisting—in the name of the equality of each state of the Union to run its own affairs, all that was really at stake —it is said—was whether or not the rising industrial north should rule the American roost. 'Equality', it is argued, is just a highly emotive word, whose favourable force can be attached by ingenious minds to anything—even to the slave-holding southern states of a century ago, or to the racially discriminating southern states of now. And up to a point all this is true. 'Equality' is a strongly emotive word; it can be attached to causes just as arbitrarily as, in the sceptic's example, 'free' was attached to a brand of tea; this process of attachment is often motivated by naked calculations of self-interest; and the look of objective truth which declarations of equality are thus ingeniously given is largely delusive. If 'equality' can be used, as it was, by both Lincoln and his opponents, it is hard indeed to see how, though there may be plenty of rhyme in its use, there can be any reason.

But this is not the end of the matter. There have been groups whose indifference, or hostility, to people being treated alike is so complete that 'equal', in its evaluative use, finds little or no place in their vocabulary. This was true of fascism, and is true of caste. The descriptive meaning of 'equal', taken out of context, is very abstract; no more than that people should be treated alike in some respect by somebody, with no commitment as to what or who. But merely to accept that much, as one does if one gives 'equal' a substantial role in one's linguistic habits, is to accept a point of substance; it is to accept, at least, the relevance of asking, in any practical situation, whether there may not be some respect in which the people in question should not be treated more similarly than they are; it is to be prompted to look for respects that have been overlooked, and others that are new;

and, when people actually are treated differently, it puts the burden of proof on those who wish to maintain the differential, rather than on those who wish to change it. Hitler had a use for 'freedom'; 'German freedom' consisted in everyone obeying the leader, while the leader obeyed his impulses; but he had no use for 'equality', and could not have. To admit the word at all would have been to accept the relevance of questions whose very asking would have tended to subvert the Nazi state. Contrariwise, to give 'equality' a central role in your political vocabulary is to embark, whether you know it or not, on a great voyage of exploration. The capacity to look at anything and ask whether it might not be better, which is expressed in purest form by 'good' and 'bad', is expressed in a form only a jot less pure by 'equal'; but that jot is decisive. By their Declaration of Independence the North Americans were committed, as the Latin Americans have never been, to the propositions that inequality can never be taken for granted and that equality must always be pursued; however grossly the practice of American society may fall short of this ideal, we find, at every great crisis of American affairs, the leaders rallying the people for action in this name. The very abstractness of the descriptive meaning of 'equal' is now its strength. If, by virtue of this abstractness, the word can be used to commend very different things in different contexts, it can also be used to maintain a fundamental consistency of thought over great distances of space and time. For Jefferson, 'Equality' meant representative government, economic individualism, and the rule of law; it led him to challenge slavery in theory, but not to attack it in practice. To Lincoln it meant all those same things; but, given the flood of immigrants of all nations into the expanding north, what was crucial for him was an equality transcending nationality and colour. To Wilson and to Roosevelt, faced by the tremendous successes and the equally tremendous failures of big business, in boom and slump, economic power was the crucial respect in which equality had to be pursued. To Kennedy, with all the power of American nuclear forces at his command, it was the equality of nations that mattered most. Not that the old issues of equality had in any way been settled. On the contrary, MacCarthy had revived all the issues of the rule of law; Negroes were still denied their civil rights in the south; there were millions of unemployed; and pockets of utter destitution remained in the richest country in the world. It was rather that while all the old battles of equality had still to be fought as energetically as ever, they had to be taken up into a new struggle for economic and political equality throughout the world. And so, precisely because of its descriptive abstractness, 'equality' has served to define a main part of the general framework of American social thought through two hundred years of prodigious social change. If the contrast between equalitarian dream and plutocratic reality is extraordinary, still more so is the fact that tens of millions of men and women, coming from nations in which the ideal of equality had not yet dawned, have been drawn together into its pursuit.

The role played by abstract ideals—or schemes, as we may call them—in the economy of action begins to appear from this example. By contrast with such words as 'generosity' or 'courage', 'equality' or 'freedom' tell us very little as to what it is that their user wishes to commend; that little must be filled out, usually by the context, before we have a value specific enough to become a ground of action or criticism. Faced by some kind of discrimination against minorities it is not sufficient, although it is necessary, to appeal to the equality of man; what is required is an explanation as to why that particular kind of discrimination is wrong, while others are permissible, or even right. Why is it right to discriminate against adolescents, lunatics, or foreign residents, in the matter of the right to vote, but wrong to do so against men who have a different colour, or a criminal record? The ideal of equality will not, of itself, provide an answer to these questions; they have to be argued out in terms of detailed facts about the people and the political system, and of detailed valuations of them. Implicit in the political systems will be an image of the kind of man the citizen must be to play his proper role in the selection of a government; at least, certain minima of experience and responsibility will be required. Such concrete valuations define, for a given user, the respects in which discrimination contravenes or is consistent with equality; it is therefore they, and not equality itself, that are the usual subjects of debate. But, still, the acceptance of the ideal of equality, however abstract, is no empty gesture. To accept it is to be

committed to pay attention to the way you are discriminating between people when you apply your accepted values,
and when you take some new decision of principle in order
to resolve a conflict between them. More important still, it
is to be committed to review your concrete values without
waiting for the chance of events to dislocate them, and to
ask yourself whether your special principles express your
general ideal as fully as they should. The physical differences
between men and women, or between young and old, sometimes require that they should be differently treated, and our
morality in part reflects this fact; but may it not also reflect
our callousness or prejudice? The movement for women's
rights, or against corporal punishment, are responses to this
doubt. In this respect the rule in action of such schemes as
equality and freedom is rather like that of such abstract
concepts as mechanism or atomism in scientific explanation.
To say that the world is a machine, or is composed of irre-
ducible particles, is not to have explained any particular
phenomenon, such as the movement of the planets or the
oxydisation of certain metals; it is rather to be committed to
a general programme of research, to an ideal of what would
constitute a satisfactory explanation. To be a mechanist is to
demand that all movements be explained in terms of masses
and forces, to the exclusion, for example, of any such ideas
as purpose or spirit; to be an atomist is to demand, roughly,
that qualitative changes be explained in terms of the re-
arrangement of invariable and indivisible particles. Such
schemes of scientific thought, or their subtler successors,
suggest the places where our thought has so far failed, and
the kind of question we should ask in order to improve it;
they are landmarks which give us our bearing as we advance
from one particular assertion to another, without being
themselves particular assertions, or axioms from which particular assertions can be deduced. Likewise, the principle of
equality is neither a particular value, nor an axiom for the
proof of particular values; consequently, the sceptic's demonstration that it does not serve in that last capacity (since
contradictory values are derived from it), and cannot do so
(since concrete values cannot be directly deduced from
abstract), misses the point; consequently his cynical conclusion that, since they serve no reputable purpose, they

must serve disreputable purposes instead, misses the point as well.

The concept of a scheme of values has been introduced by taking the example of a single ideal in a single society. But no such ideal exists in isolation; even in an ideology as unsystematic as that of American democracy, it is linked with others, and with a view of humanity. In this instance, the view of humanity, put at its baldest, is that individuals have a nature independent of society, and therefore that the forms that their society should take must be agreed between them. Equality is just one of those forms; liberty is another, fraternity a third. But this individualistic theory of society remains fairly vague and informal; one has to go to such systems as the Catholic and the Marxist, which have been elaborated by professionals over the years, to see ideological thinking openly at work, setting up not just particular schemes, but comprehensive systems of valuation, by which the lines and limits of practical argument are provisionally determined. The filial man of Catholicism, and the productive man of Marxism, together with the spiritual or materialist metaphysics with which they are associated, give to their believers a kind of moral know-how when they have to deal with difficult or unfamiliar situations. Faced by such a conflict as that between the growth of population and the growth of resources in the poor countries of the world, both parties may be forced to revise their views of the morality of contraception; but Catholics, wherever they are, will think instinctively in terms of curbing man's rebellious sensuality, and Marxists will think in terms of increasing man's material power. Thus ideologies are constituted not merely by the use of such schematic values as freedom or equality but also by the use of indirectly evaluative terms like 'man'. 'Man' does carry a charge of valuation; the Spanish general and his kind apart, we are generally in favour of the existence of human beings, and 'man' carries with it that implication of a positive attitude, as well as descriptive implications of two-leggedness, rationality, or whatever else. Indeed, the positive attitude with which the word is invested is strong and constant, while the range of human qualities to which it may refer is large and various. It follows that if (consciously or unconsciously) we associate 'man' with one of its various descriptive meanings in particular, and dissociate it from the rest, we shall be tacitly approving and commending certain human qualities above the others, and in a powerful way. When people dispute about the concept of man what they are doing is to try to appropriate the specially favourable force of 'man' for certain special qualities: the Marxist, say, for productive, the Catholic for contemplative, man. Only these qualities, it is implied, are truly human. The others exist, but are of secondary importance. And this process of persuasive definition, as it has been called, does not stop with words, like 'man', which have an obvious relevance to human practice. It continues with words, like 'world' or 'reality', by which we set the scene in which men live. 'Real', by itself, has no descriptive meaning. I am saying wholly different things when I say that a Picasso is real (i.e. not a fake), that a friend is real (i.e. not disloyal), that a perception is real (i.e. not hallucinatory), and so on in a hundred cases. 'Real', by itself, means no more than what is there, to be relied on; but what it is that is there, and in what sense it is to be relied on, varies with the circumstances, and has to be determined by the context. One might say: there are realities (to be specified), but no reality. But if, neglecting this, I say that reality is material or spiritual, or changing or unchanging, or single or various—and that is the sort of thing that metaphysicians do say—then I implicitly declare that only spirit (or whatever else) is truly there, and truly to be relied on. And, since spiritual realities must be managed by spiritual activities, I am implicitly supporting, by my 'theory of reality', the values that I have inserted in my concept of man.

It thus appears that we cannot isolate the set of concrete valuations which the sceptic has been forced—let us suppose—to admit to be something rational, in the sense that argument can take place within it, and to be distinct from any single person's interests. We have to locate it in a framework of schematic values, such as freedom or equality. We must acknowledge values, as distinct from individual interests, since otherwise we cannot act with other people, as capable of choice as we are; but then we must acknowledge schemes as well, since without them we cannot act with others when our concrete values fail us. 'Free' is needed to mediate between our concrete values of truthfulness, courage, honesty, and the like and the infinite possibilities

of choice that follow us like shadows in the shape of 'good'
and 'bad'. But we also find that even this enlarged framework of valuation is often—perhaps always?—lodged within
something larger still: some set of metaphysical assertions
about the nature of man and of the world he lives in. What
are we to make of these? It is certainly tempting to say,
with the sceptic, what has just, indeed, been half implied,
that they are rhetorical devices and no more. But is this
satisfactory? Or, if not, what account should be given of
the conflicting claims of different metaphysical systems?
This perhaps is our most fundamental question. It is not
much use to secure from the sceptic the admission that
rational argument is possible within a certain scheme of
values if we, in our turn, are forced to admit that there can
be no rational choice between our scheme of values and the
next, but only a flat opposition of rhetorical devices, in the
shape of contradictory metaphysical 'assertions'. Put in practical terms: what are we to do about our actual, present
situation, in which the conflict of schemes and metaphysics
certainly does something—though we do not know how
much—to keep mankind on the edge of the abyss of nuclear
destruction?

This problem of the control of military power is part of a
much wider problem; and it is the wider problem that must
be faced in order that these questions may be answered.

The wider problem is this. Some of the changes of circumstances with which we have to deal in action—climatic
changes, for example—arise quite independently of anything we think or do. Others—say, the increase in lung
cancer—almost certainly arise from what we do, but in ways
we do not understand. Still others—say, transformation of
work by means of automation—arise from what we do, and
in ways we understand, but with collateral and remote
effects that are obscure. What, for instance, will be the
eventual effects upon the structure of politics of the million-
fold increase in the power to handle information and to
automatise decisions that is offered by computers? Now
the consequence of the immense growth of scientific and
technological knowledge, and of productive and administrative power, through which we are now living, is that this
last category of changes has greatly increased its importance
by comparison with the others. To a far greater extent than

ever in the past, men's practical problems follow now from changes in their situation which they themselves have introduced with a more limited purpose. We create our practical problems by doing new things whose immediate results we appreciate, but whose remoter implications we do not. We introduce measures of public health and sanitation with the immediate and achieved result of saving life, only to saddle ourselves with a population problem; we make quantities of cars to give people the pleasure and convenience of private transport, only to be confronted by the dislocation of urban life by traffic; we construct nuclear weapons, in order to make sure that the Nazis do not construct them first, only to find ourselves on the threshold of destruction through the confrontation of nuclear forces. And more than that: it is not just that the influence of our actions on our future has grown prodigiously, but that its rate of growth is still accelerating. In our universities and institutes, in our ministries and corporations, in our pressure groups and parties, we possess an immense machine for transforming, ever faster, the conditions of our life. The problem before man, of which the problem of controlling weapons is just one part, is that of using this whole social machine as intelligently as we use its parts. We know how to plan research, or a factory, to meet some immediate need; but now that our intellectual and practical powers can transform the human situation in a matter of decades, how are we to plan their use so that the new problems they produce are soluble, and the life they offer good?

This vast problem has many aspects; but one is this. Take the case of automation. We have a good idea of the immediate effects of automating industry and administration: the increase of speed and efficiency, and the decrease of monotonous, routine work. We have some idea of the remote effects on leisure, employment, and social organisation; at least, we know that they they will be great, and will work in certain general directions. We can also foresee that on the basis of our present values some of those effects will be good, some bad. The efficiency of the new techniques is to be welcomed, but unemployment of the workers they displace would be an evil. But such a problem cannot be solved quickly, if ever it is permitted to arise; and if it were, then, while a solution was being sought, men and women would have to endure the misery of living without work. It follows that if we introduce the new techniques we must take steps now to counteract their evil consequences; and taking steps now involves both foresight of future circumstances and a creative anticipation of what would, in those circumstances, be possible and satisfactory forms of life. In other words: we now need schemes of valuation to help us not merely to handle awkward situations as they crop up, from whatever cause, but to anticipate and to provide for the consequences of our own inventions. In proportion as our actions determine the future, our imaginations must discern it; we must improve our foresight, but then must apply to it our vision of what life should be. Of course, there is nothing here entirely new. Sagacity and prudence have always been virtues. What is new is the scale of operations. Modern science and industry involve us in shaping the future not merely of a few men, but of all; not just in respect of minor parts of life, but in respect of its whole structure; and not just for a little time ahead, but for decades and generations.

This change of scale is bringing with it willy-nilly—for life is larger than reflection—a change of ideological style. It is making the exclusiveness and the dogmatism of the prevailing ideologies more and more implausible. This is for two reasons. In the first place, the development of scientific and industrial society involves all human groups in ever closer practical co-operation. The growth of co-operation between Russia and the United States in the control of nuclear arms is just one instance of a universal change. By the ineluctable necessities of industrial society, no group is now allowed to live in isolation; every one of them must co-operate with others more and more about more and more affairs. But such co-operation must silently evoke a frame of values and of schemes common to all participants, however hostile their overt ideologies may be. Of course, there is much double talk. We are assured on all sides that the ideological war to the knife will continue, even though war of arms has been abjured. But all such protestations notwithstanding, when co-operation becomes habitual, community of attitudes must grow; and, as it grows, so the overt hostility of ideologies will progressively be taken less seriously. Humanly speaking, it just is not possible to depend for one's life on the goodwill of another, which implies that one must seek to secure it in practice, and yet to go on representing him officially as foolish, diabolical, or mad. It is therefore quite certain that, while men are never likely to abandon their diverse ideological positions, they will begin quietly to stop thinking of them as absolute and mutually exclusive truths. And this liberalisation of ideological positions, increasingly visible all around us as the interconnections of mankind become more intimate, is dramatically reinforced by the change in scale of man's self-conscious creation of his future. If you live in an age of rapid change, in which you are obliged to shift your concrete valuations to meet the shift of circumstance, it becomes very hard, perhaps impossible, to think of them as demonstrable, *a priori*, from schematic values or metaphysical first principles. No one who has lived through the change of family morality that has been forced upon people in Western societies over the last half-century can ever think of any values in quite that way again. But what has caused this moral revolution with respect to the interrelations of men, women, and children? Essentially: the provision of non-menial work for women outside the family; contraception; domestic appliances; education; and medical improvements. These changes of circumstance have been brought about by many factors; but the purpose of changing family life, in the light of some ideal of what it should be, played little or no part in the process. It was rather that women were wanted for work in the factory and the office, that profits could be made from new products, and that higher standards of health and education were generally needed or desired. But though these changes originated outside family life, they have exerted a profound effect upon it. By the facts that a woman can now easily earn an independent living, that her role in the family is much less arduous, and that her expectation of life after bringing up her children has been tripled, many old problems have been resolved and many new ones created. A new morality of equality between the sexes and between the generations is having to replace the older, more authoritarian morality, which has proved to be no longer viable in the new situation; a new morality of feminine activity outside the family is—slowly—having to replace the old morality of withdrawal within it; and all this has happened in so short a time that everyone is conscious of the change. But this social dynamism affects the general structure of evaluation as much as it affects particular values. From the moment that we accept rapid change as our established mode of life we have to accept the task of constantly reinterpreting schematic values like equality as our circumstances change; for the concrete values that express them at one time cease to do so adequately at another. Wifely and filial obedience are now just out of date in industrial societies. More still, we have to accept the possibility that our schemes themselves may have to change, at least in their relative importance, and therefore that the metaphysical images with which we support them must be taken with a grain of salt. When our societies have become ten times richer than they are, as they will in the next century, the present pre-eminence of the scheme of equality, or of the image of productive man, in human thinking is not likely to remain. These aspects of life will be taken for granted and will cease to be of primary concern. More still: as the sense of the prodigious dynamism of our scientific and industrial civilisation grows upon us, so our practical imagination begins to sail far out ahead; not merely in order to anticipate and counteract the ill-effects of such a particular development as automation, but still more in order to create, and re-create, a grand strategy of man's development, we have to ponder, adjust, and criticise all the schemes and images that are to hand, considering everything and excluding nothing, using every vision of human potentiality that they afford, but treating no single vision as complete or final.

Thus both the interconnectedness and the dynamism of modern life compels a certain liberalisation of ideological style. If, on the one hand, the logic of the human situation compels the sceptic, step by step, to acknowledge first values as well as interests, then schemes as well as values, then images as well as schemes, it also compels the ideologists to acknowledge that their schemes and images are both partial and provisional. The claim to a complete and final vision of the lot of man, which seemed to make sense when groups were relatively isolated from each other and relatively stable in their circumstances, ceases to make sense at all when those conditions are reversed. We must now conceive our schemes and images *as* schemes and images: not as exclusive apprehensions of objective truth, but as instruments of human self-creation. They are useful, indeed indispensable, for organising the rich diversity of concrete valuation, and prompting its development; but they cannot dominate or supersede it. Consequently, men of contradictory ideological convictions, when faced by a common peril like nuclear war, can discover a common interest, and build it up in common principles; they can infuse their principles with a common scheme and fortify them with a common image. Consequently, we need not be desperate about ideological conflict in the world today, or turn to scepticism in order to escape it. Instead, we can be patient, and we can be cunning. We can wait for the exclusive dogmatism of prevailing ideologies to work itself out, under the irresistible pressure of the interconnectedness and changefulness of industrial society; and we can assist the process of transition by a moral attitude and an intellectual skill. The moral attitude is that of consideration or regard. This attitude was first proposed as the most sensible response to the jarring hostility of faiths and doubts; but now it can be seen to be something deeper. From the moment that one begins to think of values as proposals for common action rather than as self-evident principles, divine laws, or historical necessities, one sees that they must be conceived and used within the medium of practical regard for other parties in the enterprise, rather than within that of some theoretical system. Our practical regard for men must transcend any theoretical image of humanity. As for the intellectual skill, of which this chapter has offered a poor example, it is that of making, and gradually improving, the distinction between ideologies as dogmas of what man is, and ideologies as explorations of what he may be, in order that we may be able to abandon dogma without collapsing into doubt. Given that modern life is powerful, interconnected, and dynamic, the attitude of consideration, reinforced by this art of analysis, seems to offer the only ideological style in which it can be lived.

Both the ideologists and the sceptic, of course, will find this response objectionable. They have a vested interest in contemptuous rigidity. But still they have guilty consciences about it. The interconnectedness and dynamism of modern man could not be neglected by the ideologists, nor therefore could they fail to give some place to the external toleration and the internal flexibility of ideologising that these conditions imply. Marx and Engels go much further, giving those factors pride of place; and it can be plausibly argued that the versions of Marxism (on which the sceptic concentrated), which turn it into an *a priori* dogma of historical development, only to be interpreted by high officials of the party, is a gross distortion of their thought. With an eye on such distortions, Engels once observed that he and Marx were never Marxists. As for the American theory of democracy, dogmatic idealism is tinctured by the pragmatism that holds that truth is what will work, and that what will work in one age will not do so in another. Even Catholicism admits that the interpretation of its 'natural laws' must change with circumstances. In each of these doctrines there are thus soft points through which liberal society, persistently working with its solvents of toleration and analysis, can insinuate itself into their structure and complete in theory the liquefaction of ideology that scientific and industrial dynamism has begun in practice.

But can this liquefaction be accepted by the ordinary man? Can men find freedom in perpetual motion? Or is some fixity of principles indispensable for human freedom?

12

Liberation

SUPPOSE now—for the sake of the argument—that we have broken into the positions of both the sceptic and the ideologists, establishing, against the former's doubts, that we must think as much in terms of values as in terms of interests, with schemes and images to direct our thought, but extracting from the latter the admission that the function of these schemes and images is nothing stronger than direction. They serve to focus our attention—as we face our great and small decisions—on particular areas of fact; to suggest respects in which all human facts should be considered; to prompt the criticism of old habits and the discovery of new ones; to fire our energies and unify our efforts; but not to prove that any set of principles and ideals is exclusively or permanently true. Above all—in this dynamic, modern world of science and industry—they provide us with directions along which our minds can run far out into the future to concert the multifarious play of power through time.

If these hints give just an inkling of a line of thought into which both the ideologists' claims and the sceptic's doubts may be resolved, they certainly give no more; and the method used to make them needs some explanation. This method has been both logical and sociological. It has been argued that concepts like those of freedom, equality, and man, have a special, regulative function in the economy of thought, which both ideologists and sceptics misunderstand; but it has also been suggested that that misunderstanding is as natural in the relatively weak, divided, and exclusive societies of the past as it is unnatural in the powerful and interpenetrating societies of the present. The liberalisation of ideological style, whereby all systems of belief come to be seen as complementary probings of the potentialities of man, has thus been represented as being both logically sound and socially expedient. But so to run logical and social analysis in double harness assumes, at the very least, that they can supplement each other; and it probably assumes a great deal more. There is a strong suggestion that the logical and the social are not separate realms; and that the work of the philosopher cannot be to expose universal necessities of thought, since the necessities of thought are always partly relative to the necessities of the society where the thought is taking place. (Our present power to destroy humanity compels us to achieve an image of humanity that transcends all ideological divisions; the social necessity emerges as a logical distinction.) But if that is true, then the philosopher ceases to be the aloof, unpractical speculator of popular fancy, and becomes, in his own way, a man of the hour. For all his seeming remoteness and detachment he must work his passage, like other men; so, presumably, he must admit as much, if he is to work his passage well. But let us watch these principles of method burrowing into our main problem from another side before we pull them out and ask what they are worth.

The sceptic made many sound points about ideologies as theories of human liberation. He argued, truly, that that is what they are; each ideology purports to tell us how—by prayer, production, self-control, self-assertion, or whatever else—we can be free. He then argued that, as theories of liberation, they grotesquely oversimplify the issues. There are, he showed us, as many kinds of freedom as there are human capacities for action which, in somebody's opinion, ought not to be inhibited. Therefore, to think that all these freedoms make up one big freedom, still worse, to think that the essence of that one big freedom is one particular activity, no matter which : that is to make assumptions about the harmony of human purposes, and about our ability to discover it, which are quite unreal. In fact, we have only the foggiest idea of what our purposes are, and of how they will work out and fit together; only rather faint hopes of improving our knowledge in this particular; and—even in so far as we know what we, individually or socially, are at —only a very modest consensus of opinion as to whether it is good or bad. The facts of life are obscure, and its values disputed; consequently, to put out simple, comprehensive, and exclusive theories of human liberation is to traffic in illusions. Worse still, it is to traffic in illusions which, when their implications are pursued to the end, make nonsense of all human action. For to produce a simple, comprehensive, and exclusive theory of human liberation is to be committed to demonstrating the necessity of certain values; but in order to demonstrate the necessity of any values you have to make assumptions from which it also follows that human actions can never be other than what they are, and so not truly actions after all. Christian liberation is by obedience to the laws of God; these laws must therefore be demonstrated; their demonstration requires (at least) that God be both omniscient and omnipotent; but, if he is, how can man freely choose?—and likewise in the Marxist case. But strong as these sceptical arguments are, they cannot be accepted root and branch. Human liberties, we must admit, are obscure, various, and conflicting; but surely some pattern can be found amongst them? Choice and causality are both real, so surely they must fit together?

Taking the first point: it is perfectly clear that groups of people can suffer simultaneously from a variety of frustrations which have, or share, a common cause. This is strikingly the case in revolutionary situations. The old regimes in France before 1789, or in Russia before 1917, were sources of frustration to many different people in many different ways, peasants being oppressed, capitalist enterprise being restricted, intellectuals being harassed, every one being at risk to arbitrary power. These frustrations, and doubtless many others with them, therefore had a structure; none of them could be tackled without tackling their common cause. This common cause, moreover, was not an easy one to tackle. It consisted of a network of venerable institutions which brought power, wealth, and the pleasant feeling of stability to their beneficiaries, who could not see how any part of their position could be sacrificed without all being lost. One set of people, therefore, could not live as they wanted without changes which the other set could not concede; the image of a common life had broken into contradictory claims; a revolutionary situation had come about.

But revolutionary situations are not as simple as the revolutionaries make them look. Peasants, workers, and in-

tellectuals may have a common enemy, whose destruction is
required by all their freedoms; but in other respects those
freedoms are bound to be different and likely to be contradictory. The peasants may simply want more land; the
workers, the right to organise against the boss; the intelligent-
sia, freedom of expression and a variety of profounder trans-
formations of the social order. In other words, whatever the
structure of these frustrations may be objectively, the people
in question see it from different angles and follow it to
different depths; their theories of freedom originate from
their particular circumstances and are restricted by them.
And the same will obviously be true of their opponents. So
what we have in such a case is a society in which the consensus of values, schemes, and images is so disrupted that
only massive force can hold things together as they are, and
only force can change them; but it is also one in which even
those who feel themselves afflicted see the cause of their
affliction from such different angles that it is hard for them
to move together.

Even to put these points in this way, moreover, is to
assume that frustrated people know, within limits, what
frustrates them; and, as to that assumption, we must admit
the force of everything the sceptic said about the disput-
ability of the facts of freedom. He was obviously right in
maintaining that our human concepts are so vague, our
means of improving them so slender, the practical significance of the generalisations we make with them therefore
so uncertain, the complexity of causes in social processes
so great, and the scope of rational prediction therefore so
limited, that we are bound to be to a very great extent uncertain and mistaken as to the nature and consequences of
the frustrations that we feel. It is one thing to feel hemmed
in, but another to know why. Often, of course, there is no
doubt. If I am in gaol, or starving, I know very well what
the trouble is, and what its immediate causes are, as I do
not when suffering from a neurotic anxiety. But even in
these most obvious cases, the remoter causes, which would
have to be dealt with for the frustration to be removed, are
often obscure. The Indian peasant knows that he is hungry,
but how clearly and how fully does he know why? The
victims of Stalinist or Nazi terror knew their immediate
afflictions all too well; but who is quite sure, even now, what

deeper causes made those regimes the monstrosities they were? And, as the mention of neurotic anxiety suggests, what is true of social causation is true of individual causation too. We may feel reasonably certain that the causes of particular obsessions and anxieties—with all the grim restrictions that they place upon the freedom of the sufferer— lie in the constitution of the individual, or at most in the constitution of his family, rather than in that of the whole society in which he lives; but the unsettled state and general ineffectiveness of psychotherapy show that the exact nature of those afflictions is still exceedingly obscure. And these obscurities run together in a bewildering, and often alarming, way. Hitler, as he drifted and ranted through the backstreets of Vienna on the eve of the First World War, would certainly have been diagnosed by Freud, whom he might have met, as a classic case of extreme repression leading to neurotic instability; and Freud would have tried to liberate him from his megalomaniac and paranoid symptoms by deep analysis. But Hitler himself had a different theory. He came to hold that the cause of his frustrations was not personal but social; they did not originate from himself or his family, but from the Jewish-liberal conspiracy against the German people; the cure that he eventually proposed was therefore not psychiatric but political: the Nazi movement. Since that movement succeeded as much as it did, one is forced to admit that Hitler's analysis was not wholly deluded; his search for a political remedy for his personal problems touched a common chord. But deluded it certainly was in much the greater part, though just how far and in what way, and just what the real causes of his movement were, nobody can be quite sure. The world would be a much pleasanter place to live in than it is if we really understood the subterranean causes of that evil eruption, and so could take considered steps to free mankind from any repetition.

Thus the data and context of all our thinking about liberation are extraordinarily complicated and obscure; but that does not make the need that we should think about it any the less insistent. We can very often free ourselves by taking thought; knowing that, and feeling our frustrations, we cannot but think more. The logic of our thought about freedom reflects this double pressure: the imperious need to think, the chaos of the data.

Take the case of revolutionaries again; in particular, the case of Lenin. Many individuals and groups felt frustrated by Tsarism in many different ways; and many different theories were propounded as to the nature, connectedness, and cure of those frustrations. There were religious, conservative, liberal, anarchist, and socialist theories, of all complexions. Lenin soon became a Marxist, claiming that the frustrations of Tsarist Russia were only a specific form of the general frustrations of class society; the practical implication was that the only remedy for those frustrations was the socialisation of the means of production, a process that could only be completed, as it would have to be begun, by violence. What else could first dislodge, and then eradicate, the possessing classes? Reform was impossible : there was nothing in the established order, no general consensus of the kind that made possible the American Civil Rights Bill of 1964, to which the reformer could appeal over the heads of violent antagonisms. Therefore, there had to be destruction of all existing institutions. But where can the destroyer stand to do his job? 'If', said Lenin, 'you think of revolution, dream of revolution, sleep with revolution for thirty years, you are bound to achieve a revolution one day.' Perhaps; but meanwhile you must live and work, without accepting any support or comfort from the *status quo*. On the one hand you must be a ruthless critic of what is; on the other you must have convictions of what is to be. On the one hand you must duck out of the thousand concrete valuations which, incorporated into language, have hitherto bound you down to the existing framework of society; you must ascend the bleak heights of abstract good and bad, abstract permanence and transiency, abstract necessity and contingency, and stay there till you have acquired the power of relentless criticism that familiarity with those abstractions gives you; and then, descending into the world of practical affairs again, you must pass the keen edge of criticism between your neighbour's values and his situation, intensifying and enlarging his feeling of frustration, just as you have intensified and enlarged your own. In fact, you must do everything to values that the sceptic recommends, and by like means. But exactly at the point at which he stops, you, the revolutionary, continue. You see his appeal to individual interests as a hypocritical acceptance of the *status quo*. He, having shown the irrationality and corruption of the social world, crawls back into it, like a worm, to enjoy his little pleasures; you set out to make it rational and pure. The old values, schemes, and images having been destroyed, you have to create new ones; and the situation in which you do so dictates the style in which you do it. The pressures are immense. You have to endure the solitude of a life that repudiates existing values; you have to throw out new ones from yourself, where there is hardly anybody to respond to them, and no lasting institutions in which they can be embodied; you have to back your judgment of events when the whole world mocks it. More than that: you have to convince people by the thousand that their diverse frustrations fit together as you say they do, and can only be overcome by following your lead. All that being so, what could be more natural than that you should see your values, schemes, and images as necessary truths? That you should reduce your analysis of liberation into simple images, which your simplest follower can apprehend? That you should represent the steps you take as both absolutely necessary and absolutely right? That you should fix yourself, and seek to fix others, into all these positions with all the rigour of your previous doubts? In this way there have in fact grown up some of the grand oversimplifications of life, with their claim to complete and exclusive truth; and no doubt they will grow again out of the merciless drama of revolutionary situations. And if anyone is tempted, in such names of liberality, toleration, or open-mindedness, to condemn the dogmatism of the revolutionary, let him ask himself this question: supposing that, taking with him the ideals of justice and freedom that he no doubt has, he found himself in Lenin's shoes, confronting, through the long, long years to 1917, the brutal incompetence of Tsarism, is he quite sure that he would not have thought and acted just as Lenin did? That he could have sought his ideals, and led other men towards them, without dogmatic oversimplification of their content and their consequences?

A like point holds, though less dramatically, for those whose analysis of their frustrations is individualistic rather than social, and who therefore seek liberty in the transformation of their own characters, rather than of the world around them. Marcus Aurelius and Spinoza felt their frustrations as keenly as a revolutionary like Lenin; but although, when they thought that they had found the answer, they did their best to communicate it to their fellows, the generation of a movement was not necessary to them as it was to be to him. Nevertheless, the struggle with their own frustrations was so intense, and the need to escape them so imperious, that the solutions they propounded took the form of a comprehensive and exclusive image of the world, dictating a single path to freedom. The sharpness of their crisis led them to simplify its issues, and to generalise for other men the validity of their own response, in ways which seem to bear scant relation to the obscure complexities of the facts in question.

In what precisely does this oversimplification consist?

The essence of the sceptic's logical technique was to draw distinctions. He first drew careful distinctions between the descriptive, emotive, persuasive, evaluative, and other forces that a word may have; then drew more distinctions within those, insisting, for example, on the great differences that exist between descriptive words in point of vagueness or precision, of simplicity or complexity, and of closeness to or remoteness from immediate observation. He also pointed to the differences there are amongst evaluative terms; whatever may be our final view of values, we must distinguish ideals from rules, and relatively abstract values like equality from relatively concrete ones like kindliness or truthfulness. And he assumed, although he did not have occasion to say much about it, another fundamental distinction in the forces of our words. This concerns the notion of necessity. He had to deal with this because, at various points, the ideologists claimed to be propounding necessary truths, whether these concerned the rights of man, the existence of God and of his laws, or the inevitable course of history. Such claims he consistently rejected; and he did so on the basis that the only truths that are necessary are those that are merely verbal. The judgment that generosity is good is necessary, but only because 'good' spells out the commendation that has already been expressed by 'generosity'; the judgment is no more than an emphatic platitude. You may say, if you please, that God necessarily exists (or that the course of history is necessary), but only if you mean nothing substantial by it. If you do mean something substantial by it, if, that is, you commit yourself by saying it to the truth of

some definite descriptive statements about the world, then
it cannot be necessary, for those descriptive statements may
always prove false, or anyway inadequate. Necessary truths
must therefore be carefully distinguished from both descriptive truths and valuations. That all sons have fathers, and
that generosity is good, are necessary truths indeed; but
their truth is determined simply by the standard meanings of
the terms that make them up, and involves neither observation of sons in the one case (to see whether they all have
fathers), nor a decision of principle in the other (to resolve
whether or not one should be generous). These questions
are already settled by the meanings of 'son' and 'generous';
we cannot call anything a son unless it has been fathered,
or generous unless we deem it good; to do so would be to
misuse the words; and all that the necessary statements do is
to unfold those implied conventions of our language.

Thus the sceptic's first move, when faced by any ideological utterance, was to ask whether or not it was supposed
to be necessary, and to imply that it could not really be
so if, as is undoubtedly the case, it is also supposed to have
substantial meaning, whether descriptive or evaluative. The
ideologist is then expected to abandon his claim to necessary
truth. Forthwith the sceptic pushes the argument further
home, asking the ideologist whether his utterance is supposed to be evaluative or descriptive, and implying that it
must be supposed to be evaluative, since the one thing that is
quite clear about the ideologist's activities is that he is
prescribing forms of conduct. The ideologist is then supposed, by a second step, to abandon the claim, implicit in
notions such as the natural law, that values can be read off
from nature like descriptive statements; and once this further
admission has been made, his utterances are deprived not
only of the absolute assurance of necessary truth but of the
relative assurance of empirical probability. Thus what the
sceptic does is to prod the ideologist with a logical trident,
requiring him to impale himself either upon the spike of
necessity, or upon the spike of description, or upon the spike
of value, but denying him a grip upon the handle which
unites all three. Indeed, he denies that there can be such a
handle: there are only the three spikes; and the ideologist
must choose the spike of value. Now the question as to what
is then left of the rationality of our thinking about values

has been the subject of the previous two chapters; the point here is that the oversimplification of the issues of freedom, of which social and moral revolutionaries have been accused, must be explained in terms of that technique, and that by using the unfavourable term 'oversimplification', to denote the ideologists' failure to observe its rules, we have vaguely committed ourselves to the view that the technique is sound.

For what indeed do the revolutionaries do, under the peculiar stresses of their situation, but run together, in the statements by which they claim to resolve it, all the different logical forces which the sceptic tries so hard to keep apart? They want a guide to conduct which is necessary without being platitudinous, and which arises irresistibly out of the facts without being corrigible, and therefore made uncertain, by them. They want this in the sense that it seems that they cannot solve their imperious personal or social problems without coming to believe that they have found it; and if we candidly put ourselves in the shoes of St. Paul or Lenin it is hard to deny that, in that sense, we would want it too. And yet the brutal facts, which the sceptic formulates with his technique—and we have symbolised in the image of a trident—are not transformed out of existence by the strength of those desires: the brutal facts remain that two men, faced by the same or very similar situations, come out with convictions that are usually different and often contradictory, but yet are asserted to be absolutely valid; that we have nothing remotely approaching sufficient knowledge of the facts to justify such dashing diagnoses of the problems as they present; and that even if we had, and if there is some sense in which values can be rationally supported, the support in question cannot amount to proof. We have here one of the deepest mysteries of life: that some men all of the time, and all men some of the time, have such a need of absolute conceptual foundations for their personal and social conduct that they cannot but believe—and seek to oblige other people to believe—that they have found them; and yet that such absolute conceptual foundations dissolve at the first touch of critical reflection.

Of the many things that may be said about this mystery, two are useful here, and one is crucial.

The first arises from an argument that is often used by men of faith. They say that they have benefited from their faith, and therefore that it must be true. How could their conviction of truth relieve their frustrations, as does actually seem to happen, if it were misplaced? But this argument rests on a confusion. If I diagnose my sense of frustration as due to vitamin deficiency and if, so soon as I take some massive dosages of vitamins, my frustration is removed, then my diagnosis has been proved to be correct; but what has put things right is not my faith in the diagnosis but the treatment that I followed. It was the vitamins that did the job, not my conviction. But if my doctor, correctly diagnosing my trouble as a superficial case of 'nerves', prescribes bicarbonate of soda under the pretence that it is some new wonder-drug; and if my faith in him and in modern medicine is so strong—as sometimes happens—that I then get well: then it really will have been the conviction, not the drug, that cured me. It follows that the fact that holding a certain faith has freed someone from his felt frustrations is not sufficient to establish that the case is of the former kind, and not the latter. Experience surely makes it clear that, for some people, holding a faith strongly—any faith—is what they need. The profession of the faith, with all its practical implications, gives them a needed external discipline which less speculative people can get from a job or a hobby; it is the holding that matters, not the substance that is held. This seems to be the only way in which we can explain the fact that different people, in similar situations and in equally good faith, can find salvation in conflicting creeds.

The second point arises out of this. The creed may be neither completely illusory, like faith in a bogus drug, nor completely realistic, like faith in vitamin C if you are suffering from scurvy, but a bit of both. In fact, this is the normal case with drugs; they work morally as well as physically, and the confident style with which doctors issue their prescriptions, whether or not they believe in the curative properties of the drugs, is designed to enlist this moral force. The same is true of our grander cases. However sceptical we may be of Marxism as a comprehensive and exclusive system, we cannot deny that poverty and class are deep sources of man's frustrations. We may deny that they are the only sources, so that their conquest would set men wholly free, and yet agree that they are exceedingly important, and that their conquest will free many men, in many ways. We can also agree that their conquest will be difficult, requiring the co-operation of millions through decades of toil and trouble; and that elaborate political action, in an appropriate framework of ideology, will be necessary for the purpose. Now let us loose our revolutionary on the scene. The absoluteness of his convictions may do two things. It may cure some of his personal frustrations merely by imposing discipline upon him, and so act directly on the moral plane; but it will also help to get things done. The result of his partially misguided ardour will be to accelerate the growth of man's productive power; it will therefore hasten the age of liberty from want, and from the conflict between classes that want creates. And while this analysis has concentrated on revolutionary action, like points hold, in milder form, of humdrum politics. Conservative parties have been in power in almost all the Western industrialised societies for almost all this century; conservative parties stand for free enterprise and the restriction of the state's activities; but, during this same period, the state's activities (as measured, for instance, by the number of civil servants) have been multiplied by a factor of the order of ten. Ideologies must always appeal to a wide range of tendencies, between which there is bound to be discrepancy and conflict; to reduce them to order, so that men can act together, an ideology must always simplify matters, and often distort them. If the life that results is, from one viewpoint, a tragedy of illusions, from another it is a comedy of errors.

The third point to be made about the mystery of man's knowledge of his own actions arises out of both these two, and is fundamental.

We have now been observing for some time the tragicomedy of faith; we have tried to describe, with impartiality, the logic of both doubt and conviction; at the same time we have taken note of some of their causes and effects, in the temperament of individuals and in the structure of society. But this role of an impartial observer—in so far as we have been able to play it at all—is not one that we can play for ever. We have a practical interest that cannot be separated from this theoretical enquiry; we want to be free from the immediate fear of nuclear destruction, and from our underlying anxiety—less precise, less urgent, but remorselessly accumulating—about all the mysterious consequences for life of what we can now see to be the limitless growth of human intellectual power. How are we men to manage these even more formidable additions to our ability to act? How are we to think of them in order that we may use them to liberate, rather than to corrupt or to destroy? It now seems clear that plain scepticism will not do as a framework for such thinking, since, in the last resort, it is inconsistent with any kind of rational co-operation; but also that simple conviction will not do either, since, while it is not only consistent with co-operation, but creates and sustains it, within certain limits, it cannot do so for mankind as a whole. To define humanity in terms of a particular faith is, sooner or later, to become inhuman—and more likely sooner than later, given the physical and biological powers that are now knocking on the door. Well, then: is the situation hopeless? Or is there some third course?

There is a third course, and it is the one that humanity is silently following (whatever people say!); but such skill is needed to put it into words that this lumbering discussion will probably prove a waste of time. However (since one must be prepared to look—and be!—a fool in a good cause): let us first resume our role of impartial observers of the interplay of doubt and faith, holding together before the window of the mind, with delicate firmness, all the lines of fact and argument that we have gone over. Then let us remember that those facts and arguments are the facts and arguments of people; therefore let us begin to ease them back into the sensible, warm motion of humanity, where they belong; let us feel out for others, and admit their feeling out for us; let us have a regard for life that transcends all conceptualisations of existence and includes all times and places, all sorts and conditions, and the future still more than the present or the past. And then, so minded, let us take up again whatever business we have neglected for a time in order to reflect. How, as we act, and yet watch our actions and reflections out of the philosophical corner of our eye, do doubt and faith appear?

It seems to me that they then appear much less as exclusive alternatives between which we have to choose, and much more as complementary phases in an inevitable process; much less as errors that must be rejected, and much more as moments of intellectual experience that must be lived in turn. Man cannot stand still, and cannot, indefinitely, repeat himself. He has to break the crust of every custom that he lays upon the surface of his life, then lay another one instead of it, and then begin again. Why is that so? Why is it that this special system that we call 'man' can only keep its balance by means of successive innovations? We do not know; we have only glimmerings of insight into the nature of the problem; but we shall know a great deal more after another few decades of the physical analysis and simulation of intelligence; and meanwhile, taking respectful but cautious note of the speculations we are offered from the first chapters of Genesis to the early works of Marx, we must simply take it as a fact that man is an animal that has to make things new in order to survive. This fact is reflected in all parts of our linguistic and conceptual structure: most simply in such words as 'good' and 'bad', by which anything whatever can be accepted or rejected; more complicatedly in words like 'equal', 'free' (or 'true' or 'beautiful' or 'valid'), with their opposites, by which acceptance and rejection are focussed upon certain areas of life; most concretely in words like 'generous' and 'mean', or 'neat' and 'sloppy'. Words of these kinds are the linguistic instruments of innovation; as we insert particular descriptive meanings into them, or modify those that are already there, we break up one crust of custom and constitute another. Human action and reflection is an endless process of commitment, challenge, and recommitment; and judgments of value, in the broadest sense (whether of acts, in terms of rightness, or of institutions, in terms of justice, or of theories, in terms of truth, or of poems, interms of beauty, or of arguments, in terms of validity . . . or of all of them, in terms of goodness), are the linguistic forms in which we commit ourselves at one moment, in order to be able to challenge that commitment at the next. To watch our actions and reflections out of the philosophical corner of our eye, is to watch, primarily, the interplay of these linguistic forms. And, when we watch it, what we see is that in order to break the crust of custom—whether in physics, politics, love, or anything else—we have to speculate. If we are challenging the old one, we should not be where we are, for the old one would already have been superseded. Consequently, we have to speculate; to venture in the dark, feeling for new forms, crystallising them in new designs of language, following out their consequences, assessing their worth. Our value words provide us with more or less enduring linguistic vehicles in which to make these endlessly repeated (yet endlessly surprising) journeys, from the known into the unknown, and from the unknown back into the known; strange vehicles, however, for they change their shape at different stages of the journey. When the crust of custom is settled in the mind (of the conservative, as what must be retained, or of the revolutionary, as what must be imposed), our value words take on, to some degree, the shape of faith. The gap between truth or goodness in themselves and what, in particular, is believed or done, seems to the people concerned to have been well and truly closed: the relevant judgments appear to them as both informative and necessary. And the fact is that it is only because our judgments do so solidify that we have ground on which we can go forward; our previous judgments form the length of track on which we run to form another. But then—and here all metaphors from civil engineering fail us!—to form the next track we have to tear up its predecessors. The keen edge of doubt has to be passed between truth and goodness, in themselves, and what in particular has been held true or good, but now appears to be only partially or relatively so; the old assurances have to be broken up, in order that new ones should be gained; and so the different logical forces of our words, which have been run together to create assurance, must now be drawn apart to create the doubt from which some new assurance can arise. Faith and doubt, as we find them in the utterances of ideologists and sceptics, are therefore only extreme, extensive and self-conscious forms of the twin phases of assertion and rejection through which creative life—whether in science, art, or any form of action—must proceed.

But does this vague talk get us any further? Does it say any more than that the platitudes of faith and doubt exist, and that they interact?

I think it says a little more. If faith and doubt are just self-conscious, systematic forms of naive assertion and rejection, that self-consciousness is limited by the illusion of each that it can supersede the other. We know in fact that this never happens; but can we attain a deeper level of self-consciousness in which, while faith and doubt remain, their interdependence is acknowledged? Hume said that the true sceptic should be as diffident of his philosophical doubts as of his philosophical convictions; taking the hint, we could say then that a true believer should be as diffident of his philosophical convictions as of his philosophical doubts; so a true sceptic and a true believer would be one and the same. Is such a paragon possible? Can a man temper his doubts with assertion, and his assertions with doubt, and yet act? Of course he can! In fact, that temper is precisely what, in ordinary life, we call common sense, sagacity, or wisdom: the power to keep an eye open for faults and surprises when everything is going fine, but also to go ahead resolutely when everything is dark or wrong; the power to scrutinise one's notions, even when they seem to be working very well, but also to throw up new ones when nothing seems to work at all; the power to be both critical and practical, both speculative and pragmatic.

This idea of wisdom is obviously difficult to grasp and use. The nature of the difficulty appears from the peculiar way in which the idea relates to action. The wise or sagacious man differs from the foolish or unskilful; and he differs by having a kind of knowledge that gives a shape, efficacity, and satisfactoriness to all his enterprises which the other's enterprises lack. But what does he know, and how does it have those effects? Take one aspect of it: that of keeping an eye open for faults and surprises even when everything is going fine. What does that mean? I find something new and which—as we say—is just what I was looking for; it may be a new hobby, friendship, technique, pleasure, job, theory, or whatever else. Naturally I make the most of it, riding it for what it is worth; as far as that goes, the wise and the foolish take, and must take, a common course. But the wise man, as he takes it, will also take another too; almost from the moment that he engages in the line of action that the novelty has opened up he begins to listen—no matter how discreetly—for the first, faint breath of its successor. This listening must, at first, be most discreet; if, Hamlet-like, we begin to strain our ears for the next tune of life from the first note of the first bar of the present one, then we shall never let ourselves engage at all, and we shall find that, in the end, we can only escape our agonising apathy, as Hamlet did, by whirling words and unbridled impulse. So engage we must; and yet not unconditionally; for if we neither listen to the future, nor therefore gently modulate the present to admit its distant but still rising strains, our impetuosity will snap one theme of action before another is prepared. We must therefore—and to the full!—enjoy our pleasures and our hobbies, deepen our friendships, exploit our techniques and our jobs, and squeeze all the logical juice out of our theories; but, as we do so, we must listen, more and more attentively, for what comes next. That is the condition of achievement and fulfilment; a main part of wisdom. And one can grow in wisdom; one can learn to listen for the future with more discretion; neither too keenly, nor too carelessly. But—and this is the difficulty of the concept—while one can thus point clearly enough to those twin possibilities of failure, it seems impossible to give a positive description of success. A doctor can determine, precisely and objectively, the right dose of drug, for a given disease or a given patient; he can therefore prescribe; and someone else can act on his prescription just as well as he can do himself. But while we can give a name to the right amount of attention to lend to the future, and while this is a useful thing to do, since it draws attention to an important issue, we cannot specify, in positive terms, what we have named, and cannot therefore lay down positive rules by following which it can be realised; in a specially strict sense, the application of the word must be judged by each person who applies it. And the same is true of the other parts of wisdom; for example, of the right degree of resoluteness (neither faintness nor obstinacy) with which we pursue a theme that does not seem to work; or of the right degree of imaginativeness (neither pedestrian nor cloudy) with which we spark off novel possibilities. It is not only that 'wise', like 'free', is an absolute value, whose descriptive implications must therefore be determined in and by each context of its use; and not only that its descriptive implications involve vague terms; but that—as this discussion illustrates—one seems to be forced back on nothing better than metaphor in order to catch even a trace of their elusive subjectivity.

Thus the concept of wisdom raises as many problems as it solves—and what would life be like if it did not. But still it does seem to solve some, or anyway to begin to do so; it seems to bring all the knotty points of this argument together, and, by so doing, to begin to make them clear. By revealing a pattern in the lives of men which, though their awareness of it may be dim, persists in each of them through every clash of doubt and dogma, it enables us to see not only how it is possible that two opponents, though monsters in each other's eyes, can remain men in ours, but also how, with time and tact and patience, we can help them to be men in theirs as well. It enables us to admit, without any contradiction, that it may be as right for a Lenin to be a revolutionary, in his time and place, as for us to be liberal reformers in our own. It enables us to look, critically but open-mindedly, at the schemes and images of every ideology, for whatever light they throw on the unfolding mystery of human power. It therefore provides us with a new descriptive meaning for the value word 'humanity'; we can now define 'humanity', not in terms of the particular beliefs, creeds, principles, purposes, or institutions to which we may be attached, but in terms of the process by which these forms of human life are changed by human beings; and so 'humanity', in this new sense, provides us with an intellectual framework within which we can, on the one hand, cut our ideological divisions down to size, and, on the other, concert through time the interlocking thrusts of power by which the human future emerges from the present. Of these, it is the last, the novel sense of time, the sense of the future, as it might be called, that is decisive. By accepting the zig-zag of innovation—not the fixed point of inaction, or the straight line of progress—as our basic strategy, we get into ideological step with our dynamic circumstances; it is because this intellectual reconciliation with dynamic power is the deepest common need of man today that to achieve it is to cut all other ideological issues down to size. Nor is the significance of wisdom, as the strategy of innovation, limited to social contexts; it applies equally, as our illustrations showed, to individual life. By softening and loosening the grip of schemes and images on the mind, and by encouraging us to make use of them, rather than to be made use of by them, the concept of wisdom helps us to slip out of the snags of dogma and the eddies of doubt into the comfortable stream of time.

We must be careful, all the same, not to overrate these consequences.

When asked by a student whether a wise man could be

happy on the rack, Benjamin Jowett is said to have replied that it would have to be a very wise man, or a very bad rack. The peculiar liberation of wisdom, which I have just been trying to describe, does not supersede the others; it only gives a certain order to the way in which we seek them, and, therewith, a certain calm. We still need, as much as ever, to be free from hunger, pain, insecurity, ignorance, disease, and fear; we need to strike compromises between the conflicting claims of these and countless other liberations; we need to devise good institutions of all kinds to help us, and to be free from the impediments of bad ones. But we are more likely to be successful in all this if we are sagacious; and sagacity frees us, in addition, from the frustrations of blind doubt and blind dogma : in particular from blind doubts as to the factual basis of our thinking about concrete freedoms, and from blind dogmas of necessity.

All that the sceptic said about the uncertainty of human facts was quite correct; but, once we have abandoned the one great frail ship of total liberation for the many lifeboats of particular liberations, there is nothing in that uncertainty to alarm us. Of course, it is true that the terms at our disposal for describing human life are vague; but that only means that we must be careful when we use them; prompt to spot the misunderstandings that they cause; and active in making them a little more precise. Of course, it is true that our efforts to make them more precise have only had slight success; but will anyone deny that we can, for example, handle issues involving the concept of intelligence a little more rationally, now that the work of psychologists lets us see a little better some of the many different things that the term means—insight, memory, logicality, speed, etc.—even if each of these is still vague, and their relationships mysterious? Of course, it is true that human qualities change, and that human interactions are extremely complex; but that merely means that we must be cautious in using our generalisations to predict the future. Of course, it is true that the language in which we talk of people is full of emotivity and of implicit valuation, which are therefore liable to distort the analysis of fact; but that only means that we must make good use of the principles of logical hygiene to which the sceptic introduced us. And, of course, it is true that human conduct is liable to be affected by the investigations that we make of it, since the conduct depends in part upon various beliefs, and these beliefs may alter as the result of our investigation; but all that this implies is that, in trying to anticipate the behaviour of other people, we must take account of their knowledge, of changes in their knowledge, and particularly of those changes in it that are due to what we ourselves contribute; and since we manage to take account of this without difficulty whenever, having looked round a corner, we warn someone that a car is coming, we should not be alarmed by more complicated versions of the same phenomenon. In fact, while all these logical points are distressing to doctrinaires, who want to get the issues of freedom straight, and who therefore have a vested interest in making them look simple, they are not at all distressing to the sagacious, who are quite ready to admit that the paths of liberation are intricately tangled, and who find a special freedom in dropping the absurd demand that they should cease to be so.

Doing my best, therefore, to accept the immense complexity of liberation, I re-embark upon the endless task of spotting, diagnosing, and relieving the linked frustrations of myself and others; now failing, now succeeding; now reaching compromises, now lapsing into conflict; now baffled by the darkness of events, now putting my finger on the pulse of time; but never so far gone in doubt that I cannot bring myself to act with you at all, nor so far gone in certainty that I think that I have everything to give you, while you have nothing to give me. And then, in so far as I do think and act like that—and, of course, it is all a matter of degree—I find that those of the sceptic's doubts that arose from dogmas of necessity touch me as little as those that arose from the fragility of reason.

What was the root of his difficulty in reconciling choice with cause? Why does my belief that I can do things seem to clash with my belief that what I do must follow from its antecedents, and could be rigorously predicted by anyone who understood them properly?

The first thing to get clear is that human choice is a distinctive causal factor in the world; this is something that the strictest determinist cannot deny. If you buy X instead of Y because I told you that X rather than Y has the qualities that you desire, you really have acted differently because of something I have done to you; but the efficacy of my action is neither physical, as it would have been if I had pushed you; nor chemical, as it would have been if I had given you a drug; nor psychological, as it would have been if, like the advertiser of that brand of tea, I had induced your purchase by covertly playing on your sexuality. Rather, it was rational, in the sense that the change in your behaviour resulted from a change in your beliefs which, in turn, resulted from a change in the evidence at your disposal. Choice is, precisely, that kind of causality of actions which can be affected by such changes of belief about the nature and consequences of actions proposed; and that there are actions which are in part so caused is not open to doubt. Rational causes, of course, depend on an infinity of others, and can be outweighed by some. I cannot choose unless my nervous system is functioning; if you agitate my sexuality, or throw me in a panic, or fill me up with gin, my powers of choice will weaken, or even lapse; and if my brain is badly damaged in an accident, or if I get senile, they will have gone for good. But the very fact that we recognise these cases for what they are implies that we can also recognise the normal case of operative choice. The reality of this special kind of cause is not in doubt.

What then is in doubt? That anything, properly speaking, can be called a choice if it is caused by what has gone before. But if I now look back into my past and consider some action that I did because I chose I do not find that there is any incompatibility between these two ways of regarding the event. I chose indeed; my bodily movements would have been different—that is what 'choice' implies—if my beliefs about my proposed action had not been what they were; but given my character, circumstances, and beliefs, that action had, by choice, to follow; the process of choosing was the pathway of what had to be; and, standing where I do, I see no inconsistency at all between the action and causality. Of course, my rational activities are as much part of the world as anything else! Of course, the notion of choice becomes absurd if it is taken to imply the absence of determination, so that my will becomes pure chance! It is certain special causes, like passion, panic, or intoxication, that interfere with choice, not causality itself. It is true that if I think strictly in this way I shall not feel guilt for what I have done wrong; but if 'guilt' implies rather condemnation for a bad past than resolution for a better future, then the feeling is irrational, and its indulgence is to be deplored.

What is done is done; it is no good making oneself miserable with what might have been done, since—obviously!—it could not; what is good is to do better now. The man who told an adultress that, though condemning *adultery*, He did not condemn *her*, and then that she should go, and sin no more, seems to have had a better grip on this important point of logic than those who have reduced his life to dogma.

The supposed incompatibility of cause and choice is not therefore to be found when we look back into the past; but how about the present, as it endlessly absorbs the future? Can I conceive myself, simultaneously, here and now, both as choosing to do X rather than Y, and as being caused to do so, because the world is what it is? This is the crux of the problem; it is because people sometimes know that they can choose, when they are just on the point of doing so, and yet, just at that point, cannot conceive themselves as caused, that they feel obliged to deny the universality of causes, however preposterous the consequences. Let us therefore examine this crux with greater care.

It is difficult to do more than one thing at a time. I can breathe as I write; but that is because breathing requires little or no decision. As I write, I can, in a sense, attend both to my handwriting, and to my style, and to my subject, and to my logic; but it seems doubtful that I can literally attend to two of them together, let alone to all at once; rather, the mind passes, with imperceptible, swift ease, from one consideration to the next. But this is a favourable case, since the activities in question are closely intertwined. By contrast, the two activities involved in our crux—deciding how I shall behave, and investigating how I will—demand two very different frames of mind. In decision, for example, I have to keep in step with changing circumstances, while, in investigation, I only have to watch them. In the one case, delay may be self-defeating; in the other, it merely allows more data to pile up. Thus the two roles, of agent and of investigator, are hard to combine; one cannot pass easily between one and the other, as one can between the roles of calligrapher and stylist. But that means that it is difficult simultaneously both to feel oneself as an agent and to see oneself as a link in a chain of causes and effects; and that means that when we consider present actions—as opposed to actions occurring in the past, which therefore do not have to be decided—choice and cause seem to be incompatible.

216 A PHILOSOPHER AT WORK

Two points suggest that this analysis of our crux is on the right lines. The first is that we do not feel the same difficulty about the present decisions of other people. I am quite happy to predict what you will do, even as you make to do it; and this fact is what we should expect on this analysis, for since it is now another person who is having to decide, the pressure of decision is lifted from ourselves, exactly as it is in the case of my own past decisions. The second point is that I am quite happy to predict my future actions—though it then becomes strained to use the word—when they do not depend on my decisions. I am ready to predict that I will get indigestion if I eat this unripe fruit; for once it has been eaten, the acids will work irrespective of my will, so that the process of prediction is not interrupted by the pressure to decide. The trouble only starts if I predict that I shall eat it—unless, of course, I suffer from a neurotic compulsion to eat unripe fruit, and cannot help doing so when I get the chance. In normal circumstances, however, such eating is a thing that I can help; the activity of choice enters effectively into the transaction; and so I am involved in the clash of decision with investigation in which our crux consists.

But now it becomes clear that our previous analysis, though on the right lines, was not complete. The point of the crux is not merely that it is hard to do two things at once, though that contributes; it is rather that, until I have taken my decision, I lack, in my capacity of investigator, a piece of information that is highly relevant to the prediction of what I shall actually do; for, *ex hypothesi*, this is a case in which the making up of my mind would alter my behaviour. I therefore cannot significantly predict until I have decided; for I cannot be said to predict significantly if I expressly disregard what I admit as logically relevant to my prediction. Of course, if I know myself to have a neurotic compulsion to decide in one particular way, that decision can be predicted; but if not, not. And, of course, when I have decided I am able to predict; when I have fixed my contribution to the future I can rationally consider what will follow; but not before. There thus seems to be some deeper kind of contradiction between leaving one aspect of the future open, as I do until I decide, and predicting what is consequent upon it. This is the contradiction at which we must work if we are to lift the shadow cast over action by the confusion of causality with fate.

Another moment's thought shows the source of the trouble. I feel myself in the grip of fate when, and only when, I unwittingly pretend that I can place myself simultaneously at two separate points of time: at the point of decision, but also at some other point before it. If I allow myself to equivocate with time, oscillating, under an unknown pressure, so swiftly and smoothly between past and present that I seem to be both there and here at once, then I will indeed have the impression that I can predict what I decide; and therefore (since I can predict) that my decision has been somehow taken, before I have taken it. My actions —so the reasoning would run—can in principle be as rationally predicted as any other events in nature; therefore, I can rationally predict them; therefore I can have the relevant data; therefore (in those cases where my decisions help to make things happen) I can know them in advance; therefore they must already have been made; therefore, when the time for them comes, they will not really be decisions, but results of what has been decided; therefore (since this process can be repeated indefinitely, so as to include the whole of my life) I am really in the hands of fate, and choice is an illusion. But you will say that the process cannot be repeated indefinitely, since there was a time before I was born, into which I cannot plausibly project myself in order to be the observer of my own existence. But my metaphysical imagination, under the same unknown pressure, comes to the rescue; I conceive God, or History (with a capital H), and then continue my unnoticed oscillations over time, placing myself now here, now back there anywhere, and so giving myself the illusion that this decision I am taking has been taken already, and so cannot be a decision, but at most the execution of some inexorable Divine Command, or Cosmic Plan, or Social Evolution.

With this pretence of omnitemporality, I seem indeed to have reached the origin, not only of the crux about cause and choice, but of the whole enterprise of dogmatic metaphysics; for the real object of that enterprise is to become the intellectual master of all that is, and so to escape from the chances of action into the necessity of knowledge. What, then, is that unknown pressure that makes us equivocate with time, imperceptibly interchanging our position between now and then, and objectifying this oscillation of our minds into an all-seeing God, or into his secular heir, all-seeing

History? Why are we unable just to be what we are, living each moment as each moment must be lived, now predicting, now deciding, now dreaming, now feeling, now loving, now hating, now this . . . now that . . . ? Why do we attempt to tie the ends of time together, and appropriate the lot? Is it possible not to attempt anything of the kind, and therefore not to be troubled any longer by the paradox of fate, or by any other of the metaphysical cramps to which, as we have seen, the attempt gives rise?

We have gone in a circle, and have come back, unaware, to the concept of wisdom. To be wise, we saw, is to accept for our own selves, in the present conduct of our lives, what has to be accepted as a general principle, when we survey the panorama of human existence: that life is an alternative of break-through and stability, of innovation and consolidation, of romantic impulse and classic calm, of finding things out and setting them in order. Everyone, more or less, knows that; but the sagacious man—and his sagacity may equally well be sophisticated or naive—knows it to such good purpose that, even in the creative moment, he realises that consolidation has to follow; and that, even in the thick of successful consolidation, or in the depths of failure, he hankers for the novel theme to come. He therefore finds an order within the flux of life which makes it less necessary to impose a theoretical order on it from outside, and so to be paralysed by such contradictions as those that I have just been trying to resolve.

In the concept of wisdom, I therefore suggest, we have the beginnings of an answer to the problems created both by the conflicting assertions of ideologists, and by the sceptic's corrosive doubt. But, of course, only the beginnings: we have only just touched on the nature of this kind of knowledge; on its relations to scientific thought and practical values; on the views about the human experience of time that it seems to presuppose; on what makes it so difficult to grasp and so easy to neglect; on the forms that it has taken in the work of earlier thinkers; on the part that it can play in actual conflicts. These must be the theme of new investigations—always supposing, what may well be false—that this one has pointed out the way. If it has, well and good; if it has not, well and good too; for the arguments by which you reject it will point out another to us both.

Last Remarks:
Reason in Action

THE reader of the last part of this book will have realised that he was being taken, at best, on a voyage of discovery; at worst, on a wild-goose chase; but certainly not on a conducted tour. I am not at all sure how to answer the questions I have raised; I have only tried to take them as seriously as they deserve, and to offer some hints as to how they should be handled. I shall be happy if the reader finds that my questions and my hints are useful; I shall be no less so if he does not, provided that he tells me why. Like Hume, I am as diffident of my philosophical doubts as of my philosophical convictions.

What can be said in favour of this comprehensive diffidence? If the reader will make the following experiment I think he will find that he can say everything necessary for himself. Let him suppose that no radical doubts or contradictions of any kind beset him any more, in any way at all. Will and cause, universal and particular, state and individual, mind and matter, necessity and contingency, desire and value: all fit harmoniously together. Can he then still conceive himself in pursuit of deeper scientific understanding, of more comprehensive human sympathy, of more integrated social purpose? If so, may he cast his light into my darkness! If not, what conclusion does he draw?

Alternatively, let him consider this general point in relation to two special cases. The philosopher—I say—scents radical contradictions wherever he meets abstract value words, like 'free' and 'true'; he unearths them when he examines the criteria by which such words are applied, and the consideration by which the criteria are supported, since these criteria and considerations, in fact, are often radically inconsistent; and his strangely sensitive logical conscience then prompts him to look for reconciliations. He cannot

219

bear the thought that men who are at one in their reason should be at odds in their reasons. But the reconciliations that he finds are always partial and impermanent; the demonic fertility of 'good' and 'bad' can never be compressed within a formula or theory; the engendering of contradiction is how it forces its way out. All that the sceptic did to the ideologists was to carry on what they were already doing to themselves.

Again: men have always had to discover, by ceaseless trial and error—and will always have to do so—the nature and conditions of their power to act. The contradiction between choice and cause, the clash of the images of creative man and of deterministic nature, is, so to speak, the way we represent to ourselves the endless task of sorting out the forms of action; and the philosopher, by first bringing this clash into the forefront of our minds, then showing the absurdity of adopting either side, and then dangling before us the possibility of accepting both while denying the possibility of doing so at once, quickens our determination to unravel our causality a little further, and so to act with more effect.

This dynamic combination of doubt and assurance is one that is perfectly familiar and acceptable to scientists, within the confines of science, where every advance of observation or of theory leads onwards to its own supersession. But we pursue, in action, a practical freedom that we shall never enjoy, exactly as we pursue, in science, a theoretical completeness that we shall never reach; and if we have long got used to the idea of exploring, indefinitely, with tentative assurance, the endless mysteries of the universe, we must now get used to the idea of exploring, in the same style, the endless potentialities of man.

That there is a style or pattern of sagacity common to all such explorations—to creative work of every kind, whether in science, politics, love, art, rhetoric, or whatever else—the last chapter is supposed to have suggested, although, of course, it did not prove. It also suggested that questions of sagacity are no more questions of psychology than they are of logic. There seems to be something inherently subjective about them, though not so much so as to make them nonsense.

Dozens of further questions swarm out of these remarks;

*but long before they could possibly be fully answered—
which, of course, they never will be—chance is bound once
more to bring me face to face with a fanatic; or to drop me
down in the no-man's-land between Communist and capitalist societies; or to draw me into argument with Christians
whose morality I respect, but whose faith I cannot swallow.
The test of thought is action: am I better equipped for action
now than when I met that Nazi sergeant, or last wandered
across split Berlin, or argued with a theologian?*

*If the test of thought is action, those are silly questions;
they invite prejudgment of the test before it has been made.
So I must go and see; and you may, if you please, go with
me. Perhaps we shall find that nothing has been changed by
all this rationalisation; perhaps there is nothing to rely on
in those circumstances but the bare feeling of regard for
other men; perhaps the whole attempt to formulate that
feeling, and to equip it with an elaborate analytical technique for breaking up the rigidity of hostile systems, is mis-
conceived. But perhaps we shall be a little better off. Perhaps
if we let the bare sentiment of regard for other men open
out into the desire to listen to them and to understand whatever they are trying to say, even when it at first seems
strange, perhaps repulsive; if we candidly admit that the
man we are talking to may, like Hitler, be irretrievably committed to misunderstanding and destruction, while we yet
recognise that such nihilism, happily, is very rare; if we
therefore go forward on the assumption that what some contrary voice is trying to say would probably not only be
interesting but useful to us, supposing we could pick it out
of its—to us—distracting form, and free it from unfortunate
associations; if, as the framework of this patient, indeed
affectionate, analysis, we admit the immense complexity of
practical language, from metaphysical images at one extreme
through schematic values and concrete valuations down to
plain descriptive concepts at the other; if, in our philosophical capacity, we are never dogmatic about the structure of
this framework, but always ready to revise our picture of it
to accommodate some other viewpoint, provided only that
saying that anyone who opposes it must, in some sense, be
intellectually defective; if, even when they lapse into that
tellectually defective; if, even when they lapse into that
bigotry—as Marxists and Catholics, for example, often do—*

we smile rather than get angry, in the confident expectation that, in the long run, they will always trim the sails of dogma to the facts of life; and if, as we explore our own potentialities by action, and the potentialities of man by science and invention, we put our faith not in any particular institution, rule, or theory, but in the forms of sagacity by which we move from one of them into the next, while seeking—in our philosophical capacity again—to get these forms a little clearer: then we may find that radical contradictions of attitude and opinion begin to enrich, rather than embitter, our relations with ourselves and other men; and we may hope that what is happening in us is also happening at large.

Philosophy is a search for the utmost simplicity by the utmost sophistication. Is that mistaken? Or crazy? But, anyway, the philosopher does not choose his life, any more than does the artist (or the crook?). He finds himself committed, willy-nilly, to an analytical existence; he is rewarded by those moments when his concepts, refined by years of passionate investigation, no longer stand, like walls, between himself and his neighbour and the world, but, like daylight, bring them all together; and his inspiration is the hope—or the illusion!—that some day, somehow, those moments of light, tagging on to one another, may become the way things are.

NOTE ON PART I

The object of this Part is not, of course, to expound ideologies, but only to remind the reader of what they are like; and since it proved impossible to find ready-made specimens covering concisely the necessary range of topics, the author has—he hopes realistically—filled the gaps.

In Chapter 1, *The Marxist*, pp. 17–25 are the work of the author, but are studded with remarks drawn from Marx's writings; pp. 25 (first paragraph) –31 are the concluding pages of Engels' tract *Socialism: Utopian and Scientific*. The reader who wishes to get a fuller impression of Marxist ideology should read, for a start, *The Communist Manifesto* and *Marx's Sociological Writings* (ed. Bottomore & Rubel, Pelican Books 1963). The Soviet Embassy supplies pamphlets in which Marxist principles are applied to current problems.

Chapter 2, *The Catholic*, apart from the opening paragraphs and one or two in the middle, follows closely Pope John XXIII's two encyclicals *Mater et Magistra* (on social problems) and *Pacem in Terris* (on the problem of peace). Earlier papal encyclicals on these problems, and tracts expounding all aspects of Catholic doctrine, are available from The Catholic Truth Society.

Chapter 3, *The Democrat*, consists simply of quotations from the writings and speeches of the American Presidents whose names are given in the text. The quotations have been taken from: *Thomas Jefferson on Democracy* (ed. Padover. Pelican Books, New York, 1946), pp. 13, 108, 18, 87, 37, 160, 101, 98; *Letters and Speeches of Abraham Lincoln* (Everyman Edition) pp. 153, 55, 66, 64, 86, 259; *A Cross Roads of Freedom* (The 1912 Campaign Speeches of Woodrow Wilson, ed. Davidson, Yale 1956) pp. 238, 495, 89, 78, 520, 190; *Nothing to Fear* (Selected Address of F. D. Roosevelt, ed. Zevin, London 1947) pp. 69, 90, 91, 87; and Kennedy's *Inaugural Address*, which is printed in full.

It goes without saying that all three parties will feel that their views have been misrepresented by these chapters. The serious reader is therefore urged to go back to the originals and to reconsider the theories that have been put forward here in the light of what he finds.